MAKING SIMPLE CLOTHES

Making Simple Clothes

The structure and
development of clothes
from other cultures

Ida Hamre and
Hanne Meedom

Adam & Charles Black · London

A & C Black (Publishers) Limited
35 Bedford Row, London WC1R 4JH

© 1980 (English text) A & C Black Limited
© 1978 Ida Hamre and Hanne Meedom

ISBN 0 7136 2051 x

Translated from the Danish by Bente Jacobsen.
First published in this edition 1980
Originally published by Borgens Forlag,
Copenhagen, with the title *Tøj og Funktion*

All rights reserved. No part of this publication
may be reproduced, stored in a retrieval system, or
transmitted in any form or by any means,
electronic, mechanical, photocopying, recording
or otherwise, without the prior permission of
A & C Black (Publishers) Ltd

Hamre, Ida
 Making simple clothes.
 1. Dressmaking
 I. Title II. Meedom, Hanne
 646.4   TT515
 ISBN 0-7136-2051-x

Filmset and Printed in Great Britain by
BAS Printers Limited, Over Wallop, Hampshire

List of contents

Introduction 7
Clothes and man 9
Classification of simple forms of clothing 12
Flat and three-dimensional shapes 15
The basic shape 17
Analyses 18
Clothes and their function 67
The function of the basic shape 72
Drawing the basic shape 73
Variations on the basic shape 83
Drawing the variations 90
Examples 96
Introduction to a method of working 106
Measurement diagrams 112
Index 113

Introduction

It has long been a characteristic of fashion in dress to reject the familiar and conventional in favour of something different and eye-catching. Among the myriad new shapes and new garments appearing regularly on the fashion scene are many with a clear ethnic derivation—one season it may be kimonos from Japan, another jellabas from the Middle East or ponchos from South America. Can these original, everyday articles of clothing, utterly functional in their own idiom, be popularly adapted without ruthless and vulgar exploitation of the products of other cultures? The answer is yes, but only through understanding of the development of the original shape and the cultural stresses that produced it.

This book takes the question and answer above as its starting point. It aims at providing an insight into the origins of certain garments, and at furthering an understanding of the concept of form—an understanding which, along the way, may also stimulate new ideas in making clothes and using fabrics. In an industrial society, above all, special importance and value should be attached to hand-made and home-made articles and the fostering of modern craft techniques. In the process we can learn from the applied art of other cultures through photographs, museums and personal observation. The theme of the book is how to design and make simple, functional clothes—clothes which are created on the basis of quadrangular shapes. In order for us to understand what form is about, we have to create it for ourselves—and investigating the cultural background will help us to understand why a particular garment form developed the way it did. Ten different garment types, originating in various cultural backgrounds, are described here. Because of their distinct shapes and varying degrees of complexity they pose fundamental questions about form, so we can learn from them and then use them as a basis for further adaptation. The main technique used is sewing, but the types of garment dealt with can also be adapted for knitting, weaving, crochet etc. The simplest shapes are also particularly suitable for decoration with embroidery, textile printing, batik, appliqué work or fabric painting.

Because the book covers quite basic ideas on the design of clothing, it should be read right through before specific portions are used for reference, although it is also organised to encourage selection of and experiment with individual models. For the non-specialist with a reasonable grounding in sewing techniques, it should provide enough basic information and ideas to enable him or her to create simple, traditional garments that are functional and culturally accurate.

Most of the clothes discussed can be worn by both sexes, young and old. We hope that the book will help readers to discover and invent for themselves.

IDA HAMRE AND HANNE MEEDOM   1977

Clothes and man

Are clothes a cover one protects, hides, exhibits, or manifests oneself in? Perhaps we wear clothes merely from force of habit—or because the shops and magazines want us to. Do we buy clothes to please others, out of self-centredness, or just for fun?

It has been said that the desire to buy can develop into an illness. The clothes-buying urge of our time has been called the 'soft material addiction'. Clothes are many things and nobody knows for certain how they came into existence. Broby-Johansen, for example, is of the opinion that the painting of the body was the precursor of clothes worn as a decoration and that man put on the skins of animals as a camouflage in order to get within shooting range of them. In *The Ways of Culture* Kai Birket-Smith suggests that clothes were worn chiefly for reasons of sex appeal and refers to the oldest article of clothing, the loincloth, whose purpose was to emphasise by hiding.

Everybody agrees, however, that clothes have also been worn as a protection against the sun and the cold, as a cultic accessory, or to emphasise social rank.

There are, then, many reasons why we wear clothes, just as there are many sorts of clothes. Those we deal with here are functional clothes, clothes which fit body and temperament. We are interested in clothes which are beautiful, clothes which are suitable for working in, well-made clothes which will not make us want to throw them away or alter them before they are worn out.

The fact that an article of clothing is the craze of the moment, or is expensive, does not always mean that it is of superior quality. There seems little reason to waste time and raw materials in an endless search for new fabrics and styles. This point of view is gaining ground and many people have stopped wearing traditional Western clothes. Instead they buy or bring back garments from far-off countries. A similar internationalisation, and an ensuing mixture of styles, is taking place in many other fields, so much so that it is possible to foresee a future in which original cultural features will have been effaced and nobody will really know from where they originated and what was mixed with what.

We can interpret this mixture of styles as a sign of solidarity, or ascribe romantic motives to it. Some people find Western clothes too boring and regard them as manifestations of a way of life which is too limited.

It may well be, too, that these original articles of clothing fulfil a need for simplification and self-expression. Clothes with a simple cut or shape often provide greater scope for personal statements in colour combinations or actual material. Finally, simply shaped and comparatively loose-fitting clothes are easy to move in, while a close-fitting garment can often only be constricting, unless the fabric is very elastic. As the body is a variable, organic entity such a garment easily becomes a pretext for not moving.

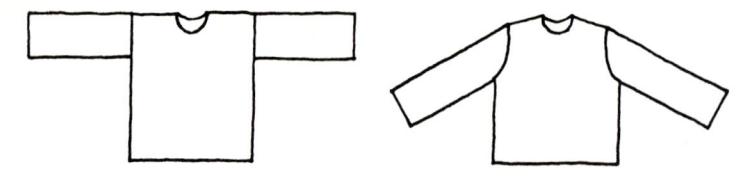

Figure 1.

European fashion has passed through many ideals of style which have had nothing to do with the natural shapes of the body. During the Gothic period straight, soaring lines were predominant, during the Renaissance it was the circle and the square, during the Baroque period the oval, and so on.

At times man has had to do positive violence to the body to attain his objective. From Europe we know of bustles, corsets and stays. From other parts of the world we can mention Chinese foot-binding and African plate-lips. Functionalism has tried to clarify the true purpose of clothes but the big fashion houses continue to dictate an A-line, an H-line and other novelties.

A complex garment which divides the body into varying, artificial proportions by means of many layers and sections has its counterpart in the simply shaped garment which is either wrapped round the body or has only a few seams. With its ability to adapt to the natural movements of the body a simple garment may have a liberating effect in that it can underline the nature of man by subordinating itself to the whole.

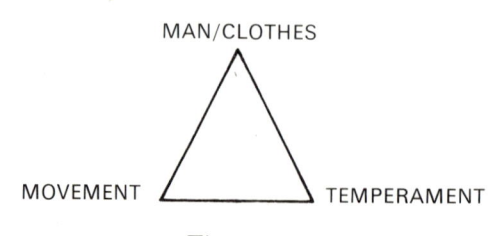

Figure 2.

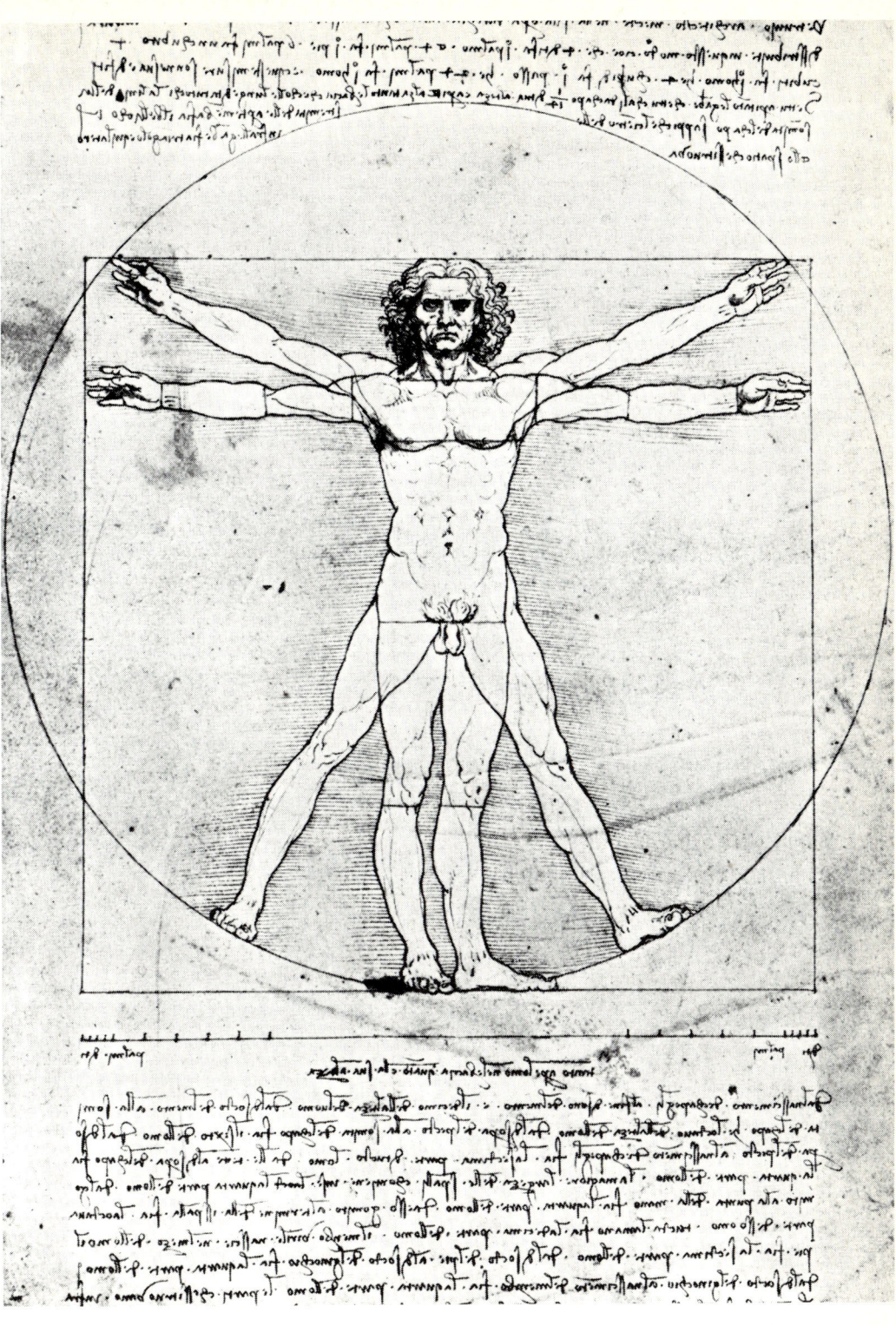

Figure 3. In his diagram of the proportions of the human figure, dating from the fifteenth century, Leonardo da Vinci showed how dimensions alter with movement.

Classification of simple forms of clothing

By way of introduction, we shall make brief mention of a theory which recurs in a number of works on the subject of dress. This theory concerns the form, function and development of clothing, the essence of it being that any garment for the upper part of the body can be traced back to either the cloak or the poncho, which are thus regarded as prototypes. A distinction is made between the skin which was originally wrapped round the shoulders and pulled forward to cover the chest like a cloak, and the skin in whose centre a hole was cut, thereby making it possible to pull it over the head like a poncho, the skin hanging down in front as well as at the back.

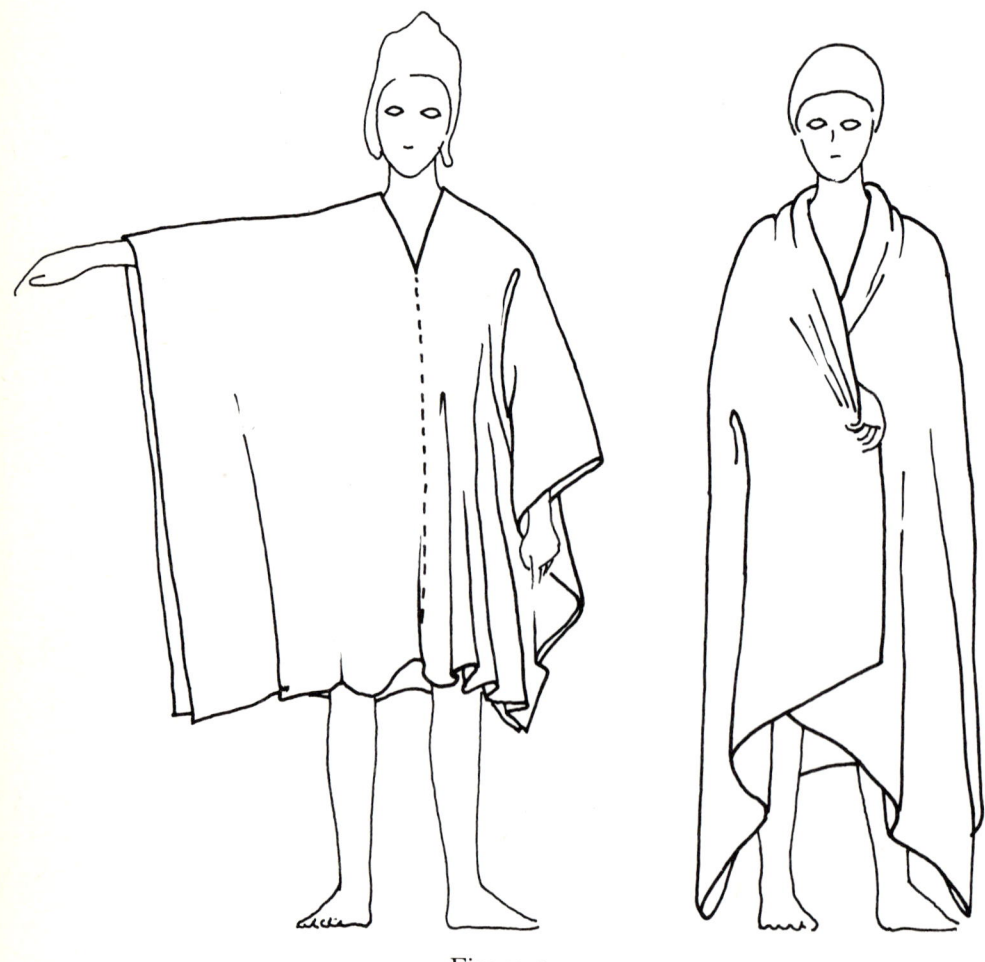

Figure 4.

In his *Studies on the Historical Development of the Oriental Costume* Max Tilke develops this theory to include three prototypes; the wraparound garment, the cloak and the poncho.

The illustration above is based on Max Tilke's classification and it enables us to form an idea of the development of shape in the simplest types of clothing, without, incidentally, placing them in any chronological order.

According to Tilke the wraparound garment develops into a garment with shoulder seams (jellaba type). The cloak develops into a garment with an opening down in front (caftan type), while the poncho develops into a closed garment (tunic type). The development from the poncho to the dress of our time, or from the skin cloak to the man's jacket, has stretched over millennia: present-day changes in the shape of clothes happen at a very different rate.

To what an extent is it possible, if at all, to apply these old garments to our way of life? Presumably only few people would be tempted to put on a toga when going out for a ride on the moped.

What advantageous combination of primitive clothes and present-day functions can we find? For what purpose can a costume like, for example, the classical peplus be used today?

In order to find the answer to these questions we have to try out the old types of clothing, change them, and use them in a modern context.

For this purpose we need a garment which is sufficiently neutral to form the basis for an indefinite number of variations. A garment, also, which is close-fitting in a way that allows it to be used as a basis for the manufacture of many kinds of clothes.

Among the articles of clothing illustrated (fig. 5) the tunic type appears to meet these requirements since it can be adapted to all parts of the body and can easily be extended to cover the head by means of a hood. We will concentrate on the principle of the tunic, which can be called a basic shape once it has been cut out to fit a particular set of measurements.

The discussion of this basic shape should help us understand the following analyses of original types of clothing.

CLOAK TYPE PONCHO TYPE CAPE TYPE

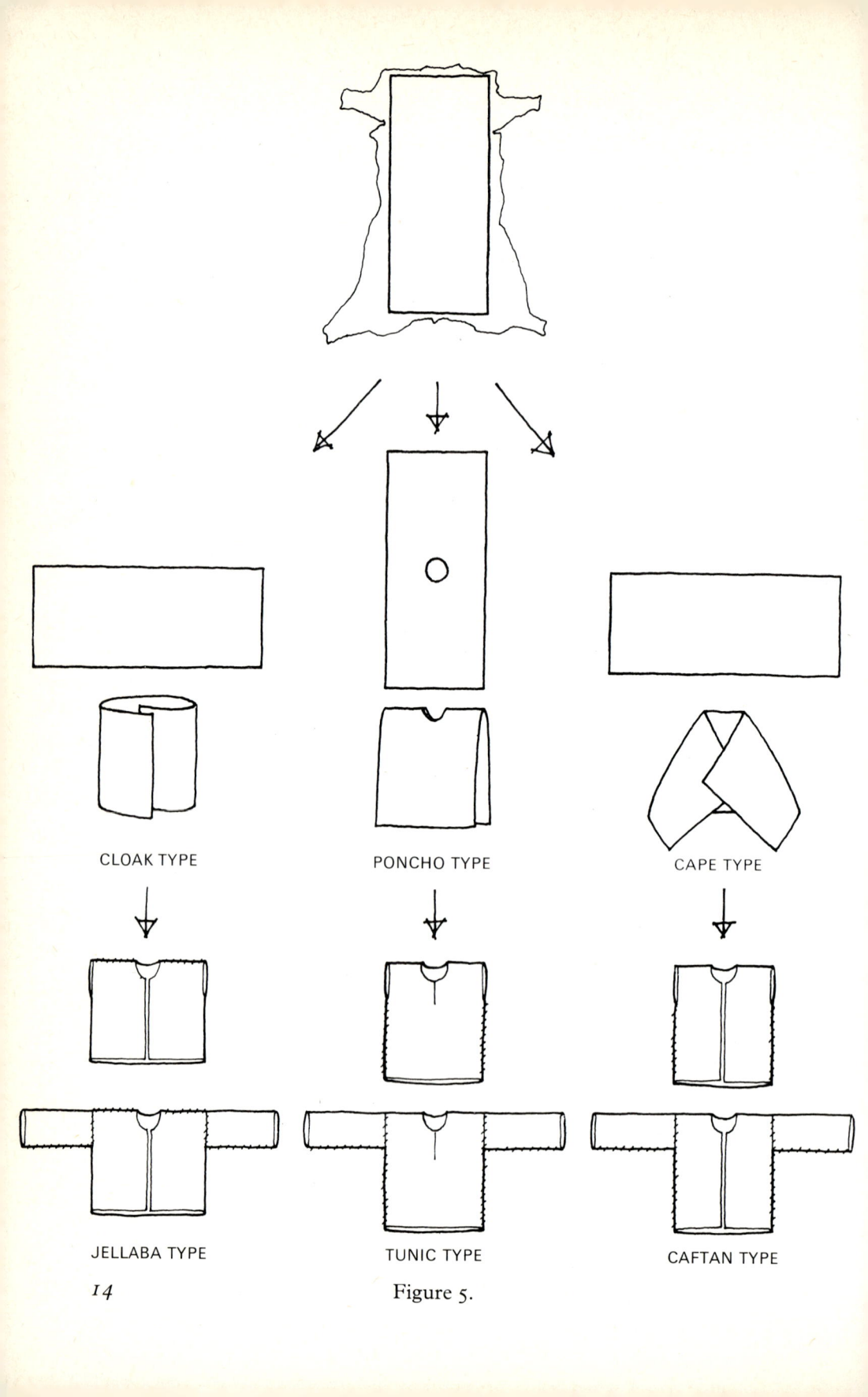

JELLABA TYPE TUNIC TYPE CAFTAN TYPE

Figure 5.

Flat and three-dimensional shapes

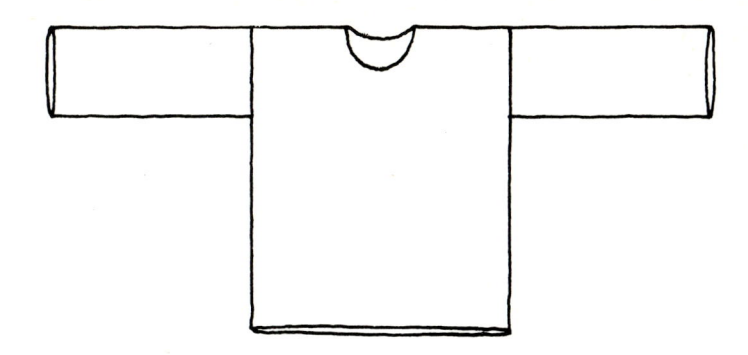

Figure 6. The flat basic shape.

The basic shape for the upper part of the body consists of body and sleeves.

The drawing shows the garment as it looks when lying flat on a table. The question now is how this shape can be adapted to fit a body, which is a spatial shape. One of the conditions for adapting the flat, unseamed pieces of material to the three-dimensional body is that these should be sufficiently wide.

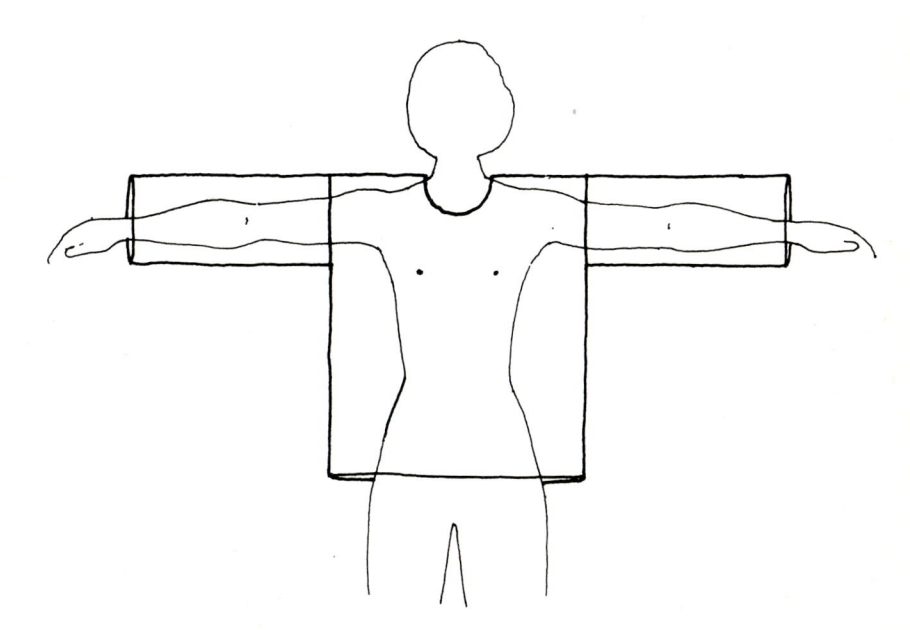

Figure 7. The flat basic shape seen in relation to the three-dimensional shape of the body.

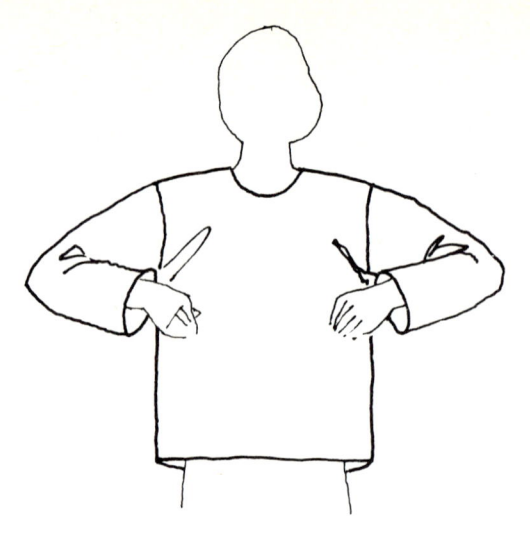

Figure 8. The body and the three-dimensional basic shape.

An understanding of this relationship is essential in making clothes.

It is possible, then, to lie down on a piece of material and draw up a simple flat shape just by tracing the contours of the body. This shape however *must* be of a size which, instead of merely enveloping the body, also allows the possibility of movement. Extra material also has to be added for the seams.

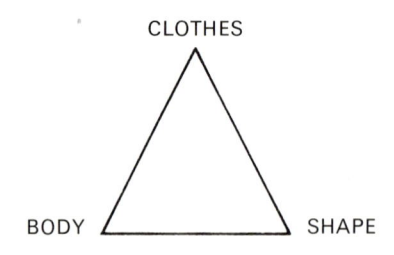

Figure 9.

The basic shape

Another method of cutting out is based on taking body measurements. As this method is easier and more practical it is the one used as a basis for drawing the garments in this book.

Of course human bodies differ from one another, and individual measurements must be taken at particular places before drawing the basic shape.

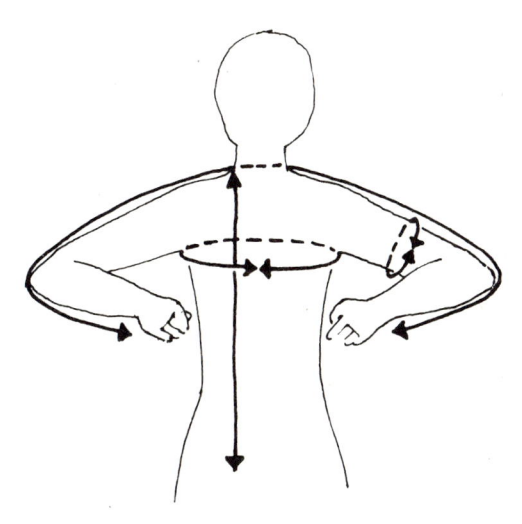

Figure 10. Measuring the body.

Because a garment must allow room for movement, when drawing the basic shape extra width must be added to the basic body measurements. Once this has been done we have the basic measurements to be used when drawing the basic shape (see fig. 65).

In order to be able to use this basic shape in different ways, we have to investigate first how other cultures have fashioned their clothes. What follows is an analysis of original types of clothing from which we can proceed to make the basic shape for modern clothes.

Analyses

In the previous section we have described how a garment—both flat and spatial—is related to the body. Conversely, by unfolding a spatial shape, unstitching the seams for example, we can work out how it has been made. This is the purpose of the analytical drawings below.

The analyses, text as well as drawings, are to be looked upon as a whole and as broadly formulated introductions based on a division of different clothes into principles of shape: each analytical drawing represents a characteristic structuring of the garment. The analysis of the tunic, for example, covers the principle of the tunic, and its basic structure.

This classification will give a better idea of the various possibilities of each type of garment and will make it easier to select the principles of shape suited to a particular level of dressmaking competence.

It should be stressed that the basic facts about flat and three-dimensional shape can be grasped without making all the garments for which examples are given here. A quick and economical process is to transfer the drawings to soft paper, then cut out, fold and put together the garment shape. This quick elementary study of the sources should also provide a useful stimulus.

THE KANGA

With its rectangular shape the kanga, the African wraparound garment, represents the simplest conceivable principle of form.

The kanga is made of lightweight, cool cotton decorated with batik or template printing in a few strong colours. The patterns are placed in relation to the selvedges or the centre of the material, and often have a symbolic meaning.

The kanga can be wrapped round the body in different ways. Sometimes two kangas are worn together. According to climate, taste and function it is placed—without pins or hooks—round the waist, bosom or head, or slantwise across one shoulder. It can also be put on in such a way that it forms a sling for a baby on the back.

In the Tanzanian countryside the kanga is still the most popular female garment. It is closely connected with woman's tradition-bound existence without prospects of education and equality. Besides looking after the children, the village woman has to till the land, harvest the crops and fetch water, often from many kilometres away. So the kanga is made for a body in movement. It is one with the body, yielding to it and emphasising it. Conversely

Figure 11. The Tanzanian kanga. *Photograph: Jesper Kirknaes.*

the movement of the body adds a living beauty to the material in the play of colours, light and shade.

The kanga has many relatives: the Egyptian loincloth, the Indian sari and the Roman toga.

It is characteristic of all these unseamed types of clothing that they consist of a flat, carefully chosen piece of material which only becomes a three-dimensional garment when it is wrapped round the body as a protection and as part of the personality.

THE PEPLUS

The peplus is a cylindrical shape. Three cylindrically shaped garments from the Iron Age have been found in Denmark. The best known sample is from the Huldre bog. Its length is 1.68 m and its width 2.64 m. These garments have no seams, which means that they were woven as one unbroken tubular shape on a circular loom. Similar circular looms are used in many cultures today and it is fair to assume that the technical possibilities of the circular loom have been decisive for the shape of tubular garments.

Figure 12. Schematic drawing of the kanga.

Figure 13. The Gundestrup vessel. *Danish National Museum.*

The way in which these long, wide articles of clothing were worn has been the subject of much speculation. Only a few dim relics from the past tell us something about them. On the Gundestrup vessel dating from the early Iron Age we see a couple of women wearing long garments which seem to be pinned together at the shoulders. But no details can be discerned from these pictures. Finds of Roman coins have helped to prove that there were links between Northern and Southern Europe in the Iron Age. It is natural, therefore, to compare these Iron Age clothes with contemporary Southern European garments.

From antiquity we know of numerous Greek representations of man. Paintings on vases give us an idea of the Greek way of life, including also their way of dressing. The garment occurring most frequently on these vases is called a peplus.

The ideal of continuity and clarity is characteristic of the Greek attitude to life and this is reflected in the Greek peplus. It is an expression of unity and balance; it is monumental, like a temple column. The garment is tubular and is found in many variations. It is stitched together at one or both sides, or it is left open. According to the fabric used some have a slender, some a wide cut. At the shoulders the garment is pinned together in such a way that it sometimes looks as if it has sleeves. At the top the material is folded to create a flap which, by means of a belt, can be puffed out so as to produce a blouse-like effect. Alternatively the flap can be pulled over the head to form a kind of hood.

The Greek peplus has been compared to the Danish Huldre bog garment. The latter is made of coarse wool and is therefore narrower than the Greek peplus, which, as a rule, is made of a lighter wool. Since there are needle marks in the Huldre bog garment, and since dress pins—fibula—have been found in pairs in graves in Denmark and Northern Germany, we can assume that the Huldre bog garment was pinned together at the shoulders.

The study of the Greek peplus provides us with a basis for the theory about how the Danish Iron Age woman wore her simple tubular garment.

Figure 14.

THE JELLABA

The jibba is a simple, Arabian top garment. It is made of one piece of material with slits for the arms and is sewn together at the shoulders and centrally down the front only. The aba is a similar but open garment from the Near East. Max Tilke (and others) are of the opinion that both types originate from the wraparound garment because the material is used in such a way that the selvedges are to be found at the top and at the bottom. The garments have seams at the shoulders.

The jellaba is a North African man's garment which combines features of the aba and the jibba—both etymologically and as regards shape.

This garment is clearly meant for a hot climate. It is very wide and has stumpy sleeves which often are only partially sewn on so as to provide ventilation. The loose, broad hood can cover the

Figure 15. Red oil bottle by the Nikon painter ca. 460 BC. On the right, a woman wearing a peplus. *Danish National Museum, Antiques Collection.*

Figure 16. The Huldre bog peplus. *Danish National Museum.*

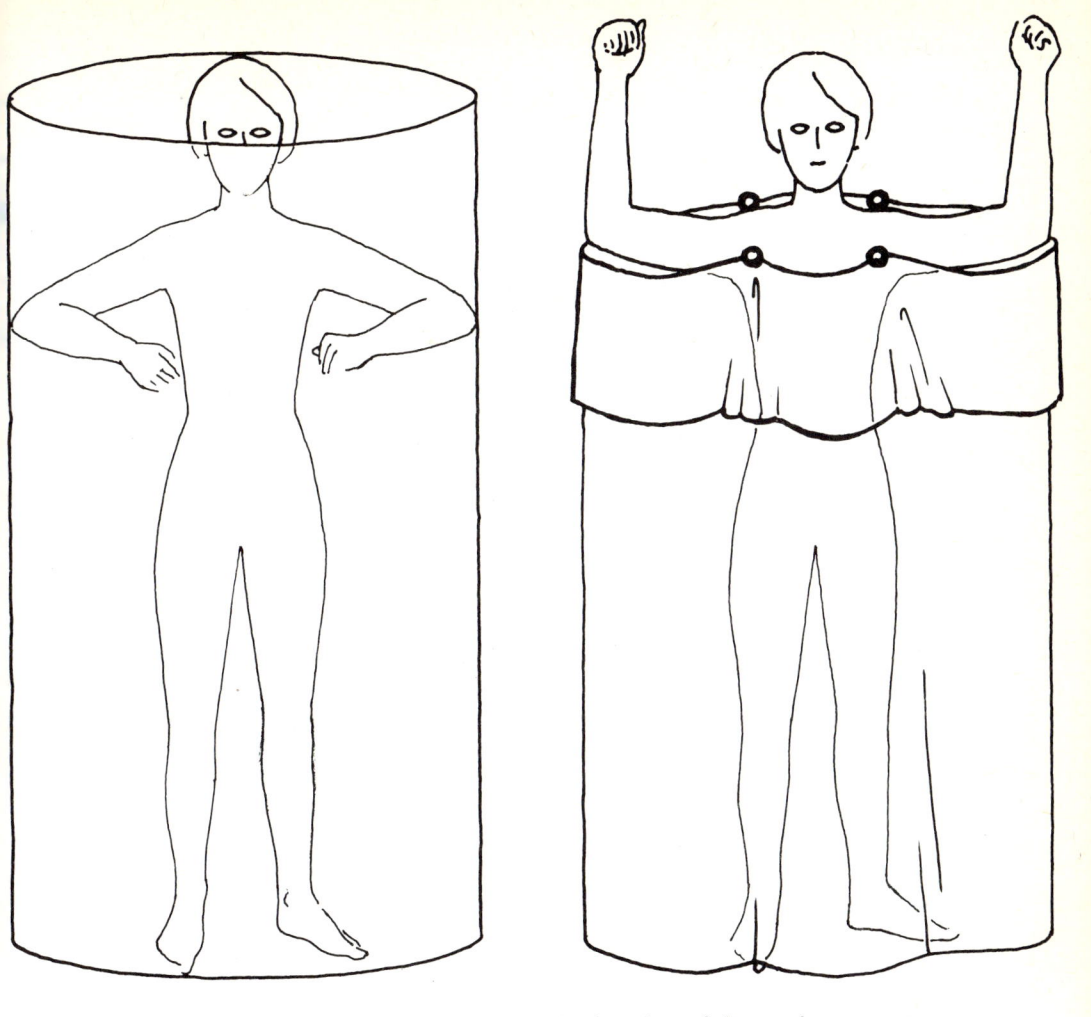

Figure 17. Schematic drawing of the peplus.

forehead completely, shielding it from the sun. In front the garment is fitted with a practical double pocket which is placed in the partially open seam at the centre.

Nowadays the jellaba is worn in North African towns. It is often made of grey or brown wool and decorated with simple, geometrical trimmings. Alternatively it is made of coarse, dark-blue cotton with red trimmings and decorative tassels.

THE PONCHO

In common usage a poncho is a piece of material or skin with a hole for the head in the middle—a top garment covering the shoulders and providing good possibilities for ornamental patterns. Thus

Figure 18. The Moroccan jellaba. *Photograph: FAO.*

defined, the poncho is widespread throughout the greater part of the world.

The Central and South American ponchos often consist of several widths of woven material, there being an obvious connection between the shape of the garment and the possibilities offered by the loom. The widths are woven on a simple, horizontal loom, a so-called 'loin loom'. The warp of the loom is stretched out between two round sticks. The weaver, who sits on the ground, fastens one of the round sticks to a belt girded round the small of his back. The other round stick is tied to a tree. By lifting himself onto his knees and sitting down again the weaver can, without difficulty, slacken and tighten the warp as he wishes. On this type of loom only lengths of material of a limited width can be manufactured.

Figure 19. Schematic drawing of the jellaba.

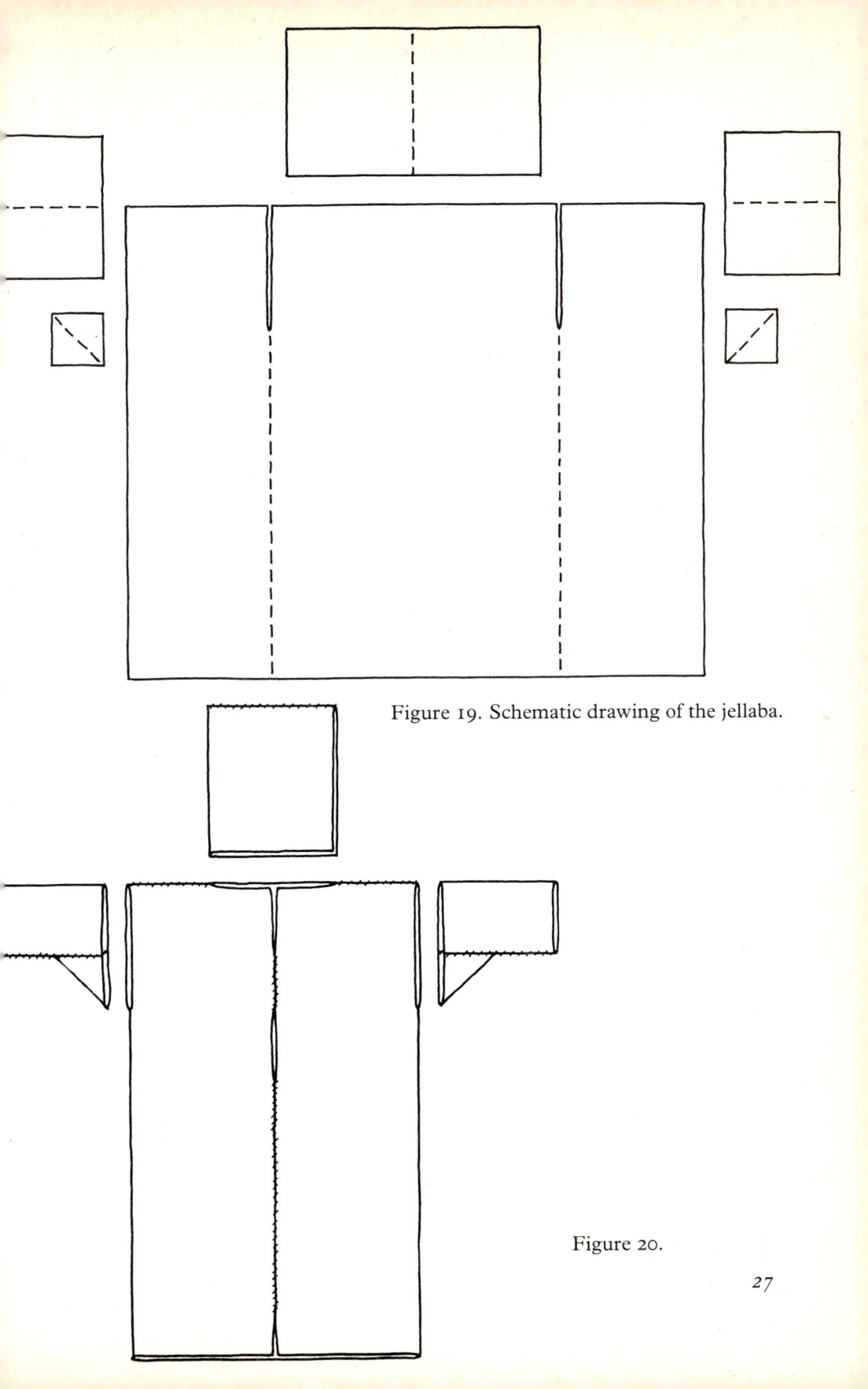

Figure 20.

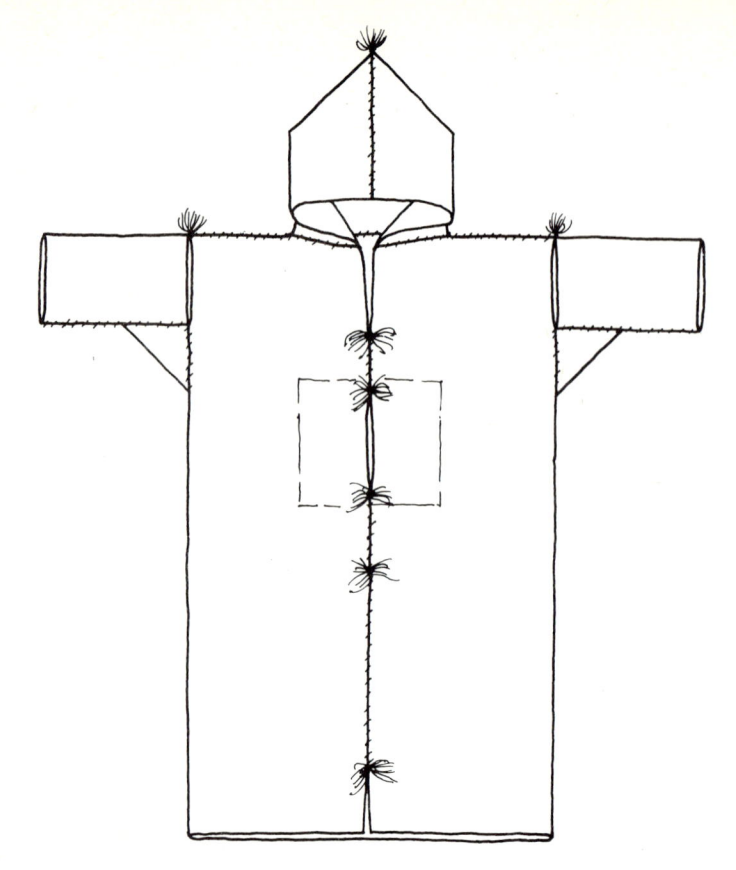

Figure 21.

JELLABA TYPES

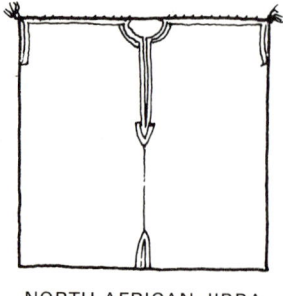

NORTH AFRICAN JIBBA   ARABIAN ABA

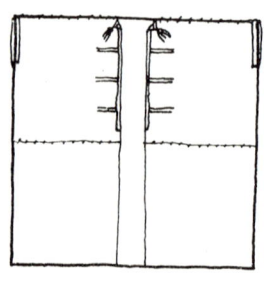

Figure 22.

In Peru, the country of the Incas, the poncho is an important article of clothing. Experts have investigated the precursors of the poncho amongst the finds from the ancient Inca Empire and a number of mummy cases have been found, containing kitchen utensils, tools and clothes. The clothes are often wrapped round the mummy in several layers, or they lie folded up next to it. These clothes are either much smaller or much larger than the human scale and their function is symbolic.

Amongst the finds there are several simple types of blouses which look like ponchos, but which are stitched together at the sides. These blouses are richly decorated with woven patterns, embroideries, batik decorations, appliqué work, needle weaving or feather mosaics. The decorations provide information about the origin, time and place of the clothes. There are also some large, ceremonial cloaks. In shape they resemble the poncho and thus might have been its precursors.

Another theory about the poncho is that it came to Peru with the Spaniards who banned the traditional dress in an attempt to crush the highly developed Inca culture by wiping out national

Figure 23. The Peruvian poncho. *Photograph: Per Rasmussen.*

Figure 24. A mummy case from Peru. *Danish National Museum.*

characteristics. Further the poncho, which is extremely well suited for riding, became common in the course of the sixteenth century—the period during which the Spaniards brought the horse to Peru.

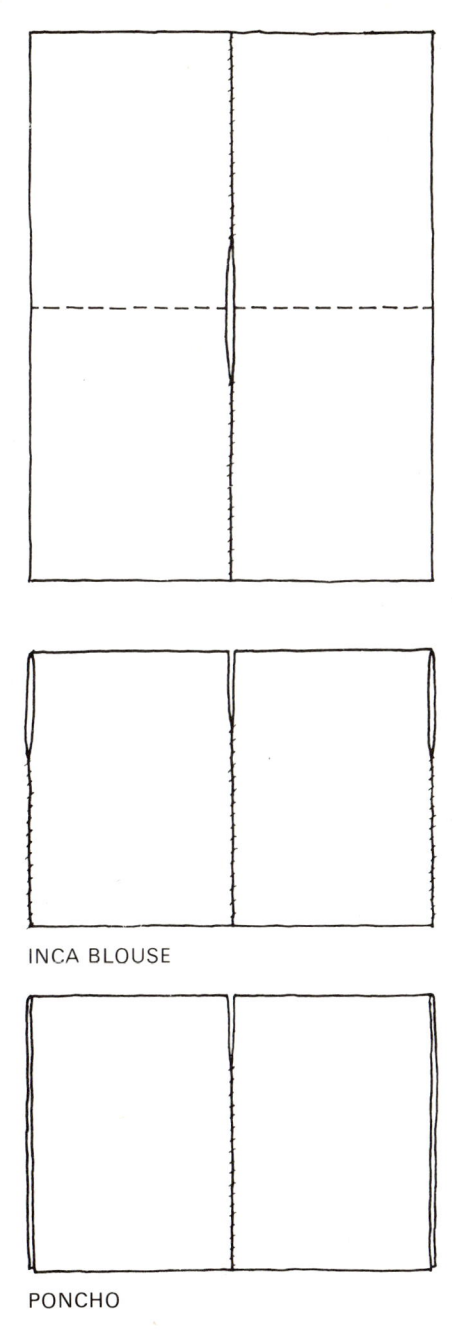

INCA BLOUSE

PONCHO

Figure 25. Schematic drawing of the poncho.

SOUTH AMERICAN   SOUTH AMERICAN   MEXICO

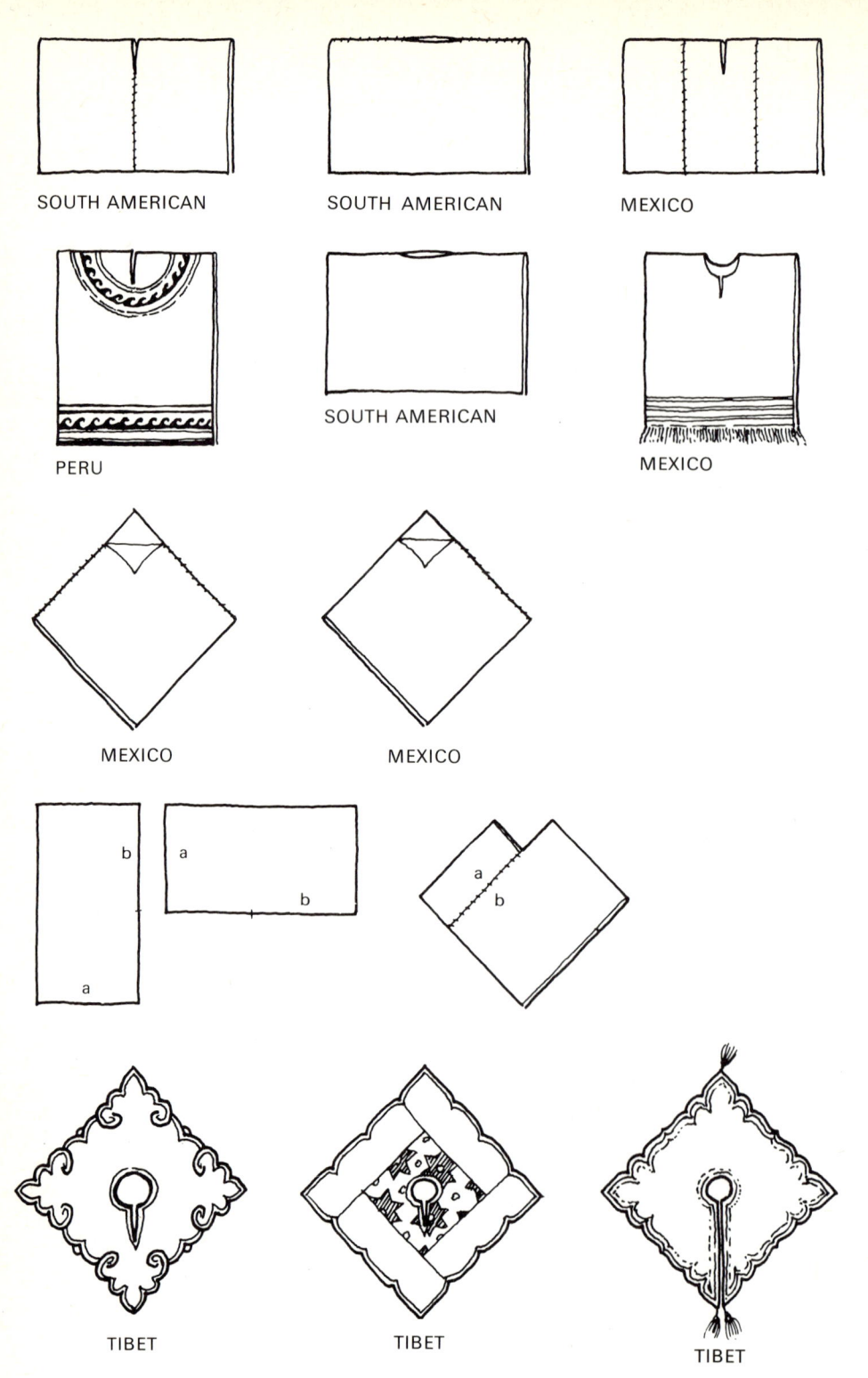

PERU   SOUTH AMERICAN   MEXICO

MEXICO   MEXICO

TIBET   TIBET   TIBET

Figure 26. Poncho types.

THE BRONZE AGE BLOUSE

It is exceptionally fortunate that clothes from the early Bronze Age (1400-1200 B.C.) are extant in Europe.

This has happened because during the period burial customs underwent a radical change. Prosperous people came to be buried singly in oak coffins which were covered under mounds of earth. Remains of people and their everyday utensils have been well preserved in these graves as a result of the humidity around the oak coffin, the low temperature and the particular strata of earth that have enveloped the contents of the coffin as in a hermetically sealed case. Thus horny parts in particular, such as hair, skin, nails and wool, have been preserved for a period of 3,000 years.

Between the years 1827 and 1935 four male and three female garments were found in Bronze Age graves. The female garments are similar to each other in principle. The clothes of the time were light and comparatively thin, suitable for the mild climate of the Bronze Age. The remains of a flower (*Achillea millefolium*) lying next to the dead body in one grave tells us that the garment must have been a summer dress.

The girl in this grave, at Egtved in Jutland, was dressed in a skirt made of vertical strings with clinking charms. This type of skirt has been found at several places and small sculptures from the period show how the skirt was worn. With the skirt the girl wore a belt with a big, decorated bronze disc and a woollen blouse.

Figure 27. Bronze Age burial mounds. *Danish National Museum.*

The blouse is characterised by having been cut out of one piece of material. The way in which the material of these woven garments has been cut and sewn together again has led researchers to believe that the technique was invented and developed in connection with the use of animal skins, and that Bronze Age man continued to make blouses according to the shape of the animal skin even after the introduction of weaving. This theory is further supported by the fact that by placing a copy of an unstitched blouse on top of an animal skin it can be seen how well the skin has been utilised for a blouse of this kind.

The fact that the material used influenced the design may seem absurd to the modern designer who is used to deciding on the model first and then at a later stage buying the material, cutting out the necessary parts and discarding the rest.

But everybody knows that even textile resources are becoming increasingly limited and that we may have to unstitch used clothes, cut them again, or patch them up, as was the case during the last war. Here we can learn from the ancients who turned the skins over and over again, and utilised woven lengths of material carefully, thus adapting the shape of the garment to the material available.

Figure 28. Grave of a girl at Egtved, Denmark. *Danish National Museum.*

Figure 29. The Egtved girl's garment. *Danish National Museum.*

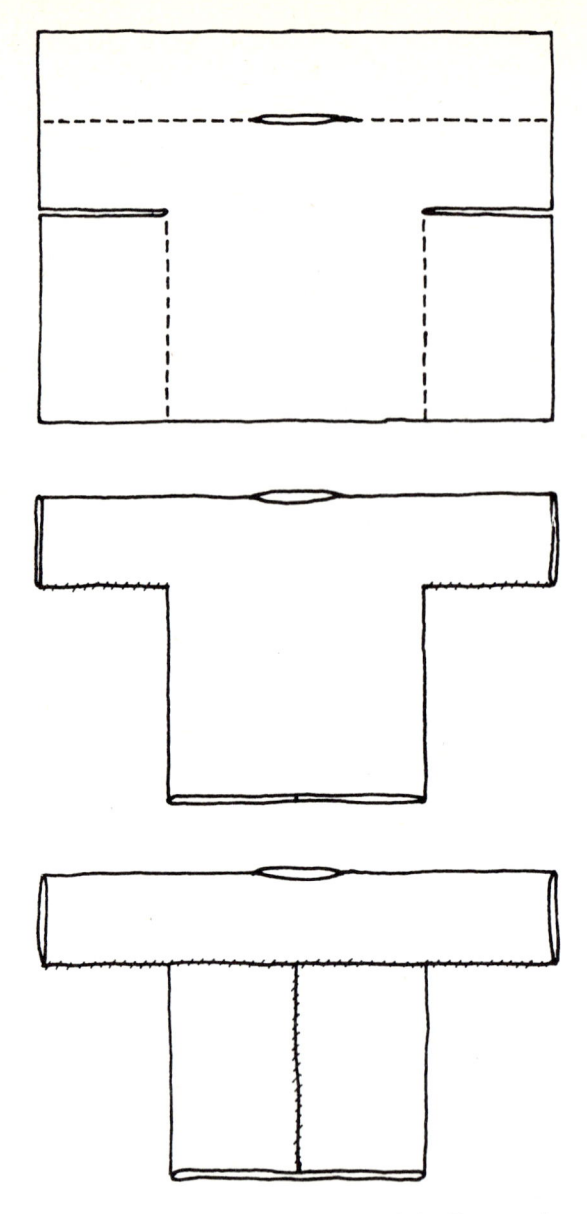

Figure 30. Schematic drawing of the Bronze Age blouse.

IRAN

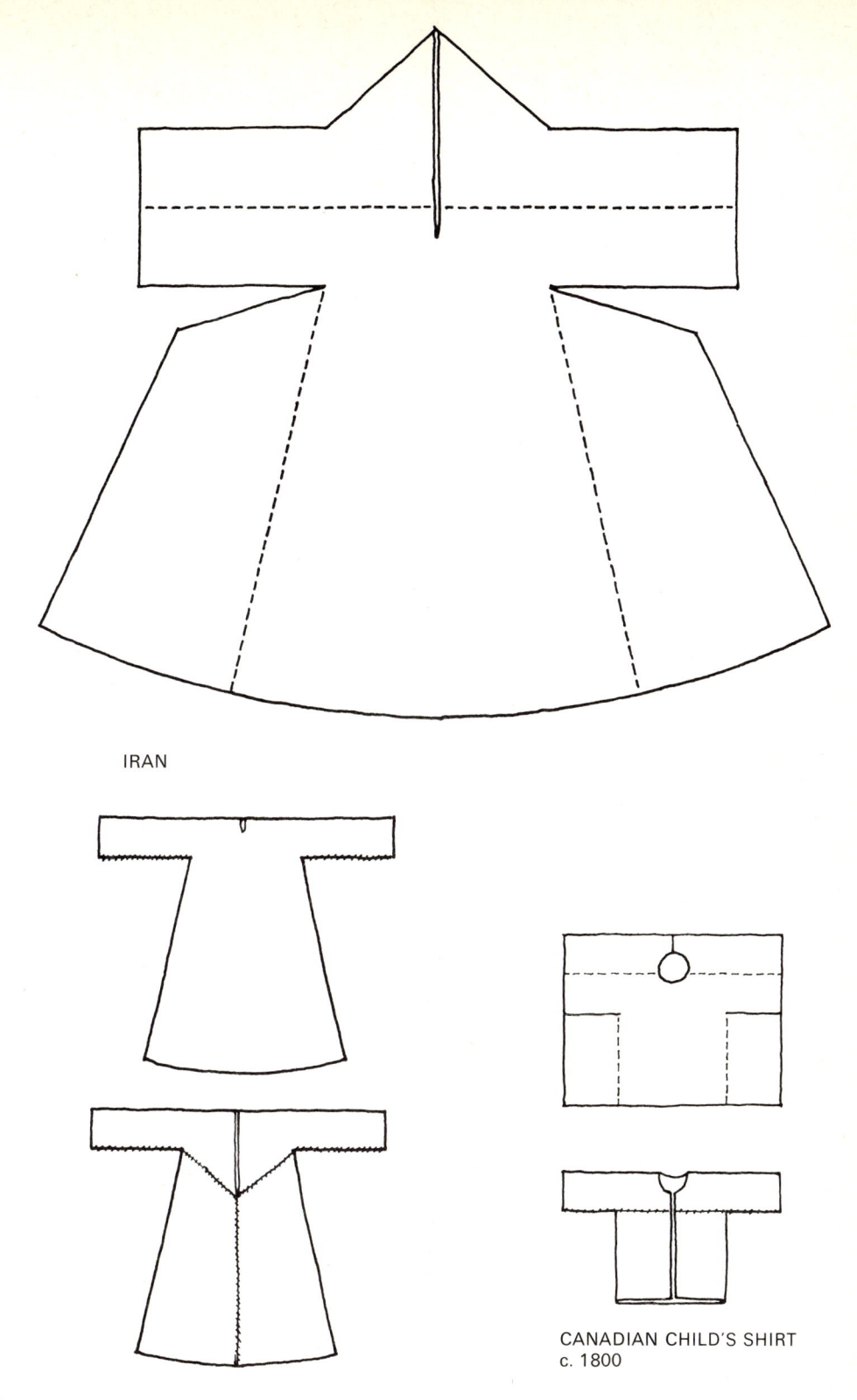

CANADIAN CHILD'S SHIRT
c. 1800

Figure 31. Various types of Bronze Age blouse.

THE TUNIC

Originally the cruciform Roman tunic was woven in one piece. Only towards the end of the Roman Empire were the sleeves sewn onto the body and, at the same time, lengthened.

It is possible to get an idea of the Roman way of dressing by looking at pictures of mural paintings and Roman tesselated floors from, for example, Pompeii.

The ordinary citizen's clothes were grey or black, while those of the upper classes were white. The festive tunic was often embroidered with brilliant colours or decorated with purple stripes.

While the Greek way of dressing involved one, at the most two articles of clothing, that of the Romans involved several.

Thus the tunic was originally a type of underwear for both men and women. The Roman woman's underwear consisted of a scarf or a ribbon under the bosom and a long tunic with or withouth sleeves. On top she wore a long, short-sleeved dress, called a stole, and a pall, a cloak which could be used as a veil. A belt placed above the waist could also form part of the costume.

The male costume consisted of a knee-length tunic worn with a belt. On top of this a toga was worn as a kind of cloak. The toga was a long piece of material wrapped round the body and folded in such a way that it almost hid the tunic underneath. When the toga, after having reached its maximum size, gradually became smaller again, the tunic came increasingly to be used as an independent article of clothing. The tunic recurs in Byzantine garments and in garments which were worn at church ceremonies.

Even today the long tunic, which is also called a kirtle (or coat), can still be seen in Yugoslavia as a folk costume of exactly the same cut. The basic cruciform principle of the tunic can be seen in a variety of garments throughout the world.

Figure 32. A miniature from the 11th century.
The Cathedral Archives, Bari.

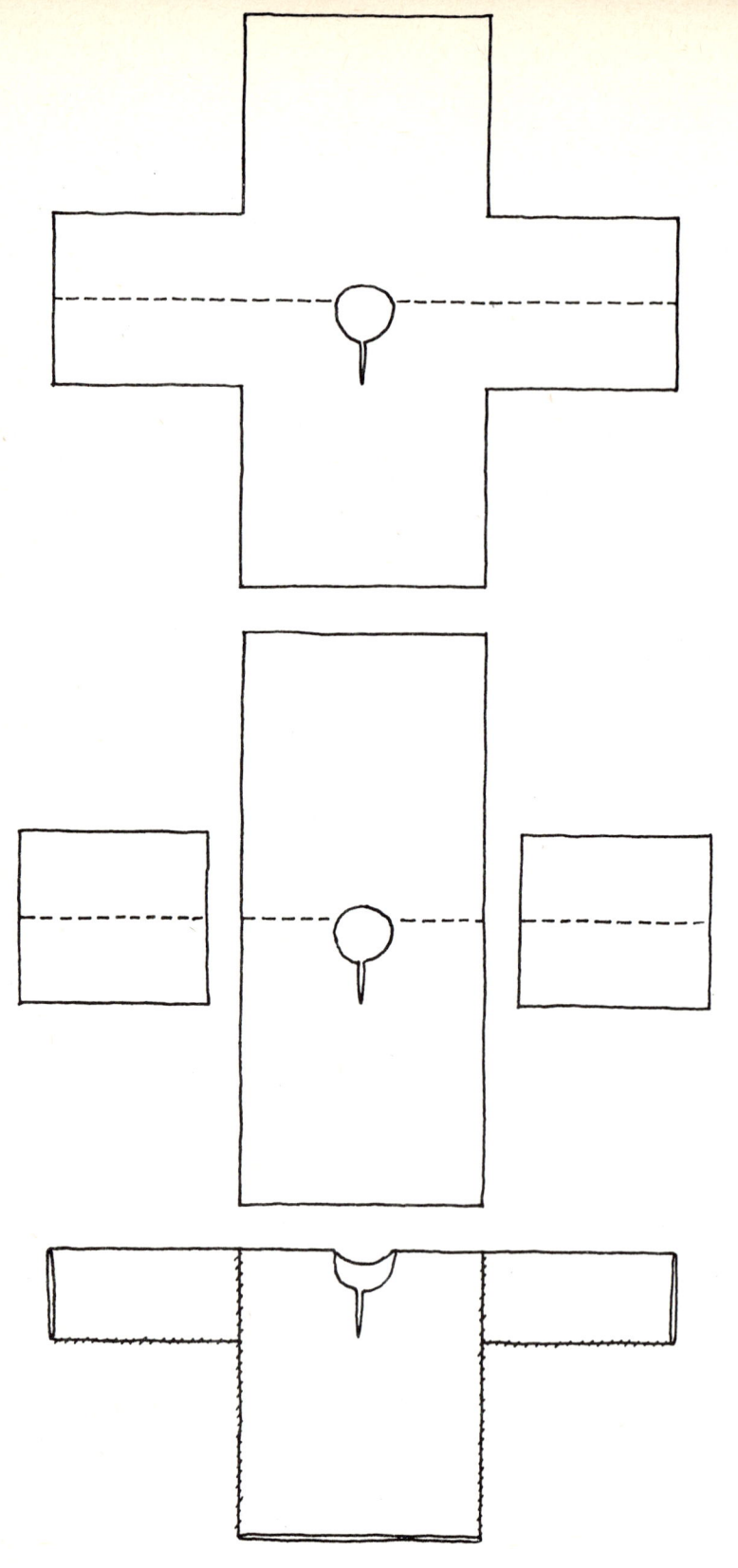

Figure 33. Schematic drawing of the tunic.

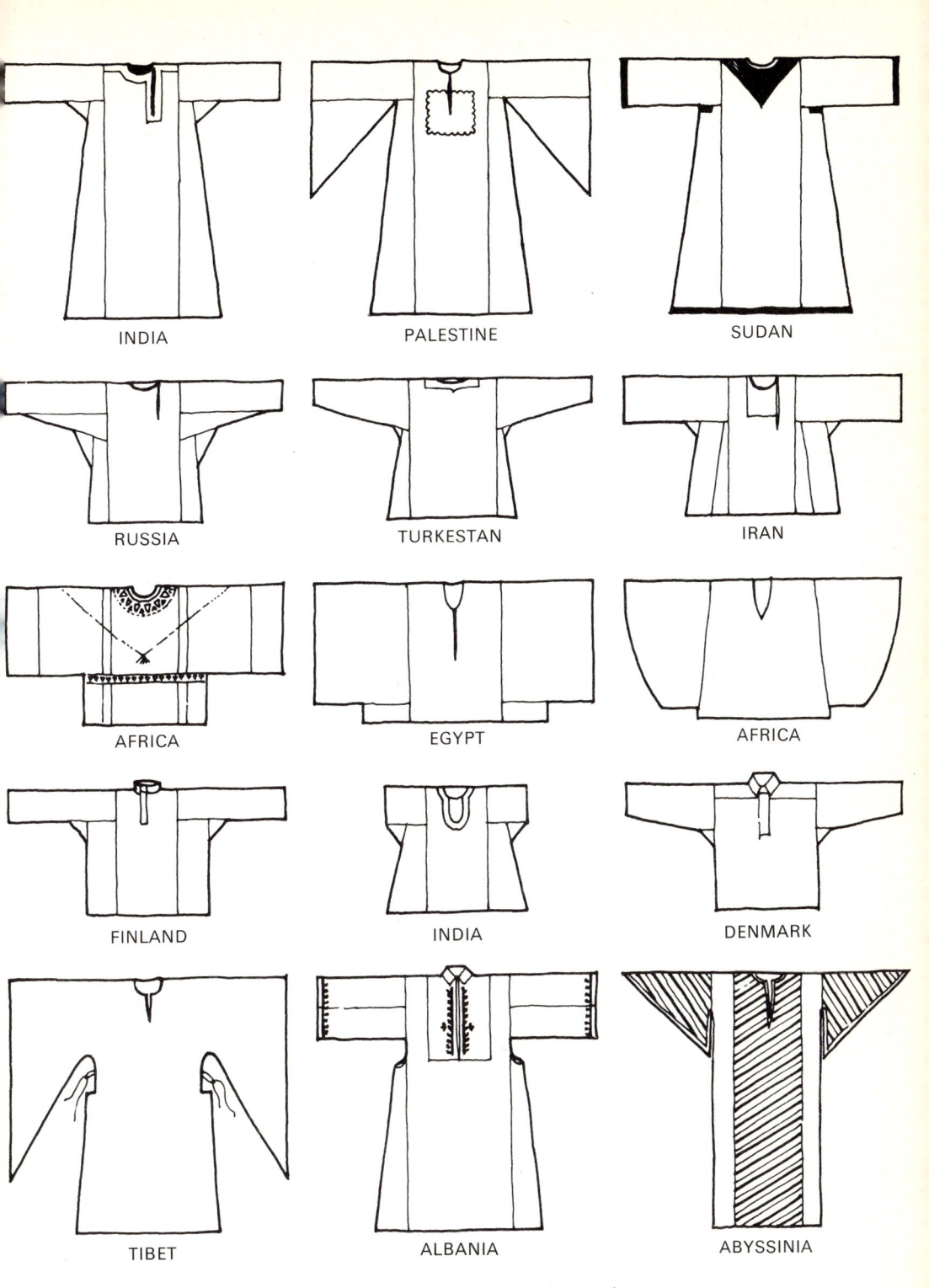

Figure 34. Types of tunic and coat.

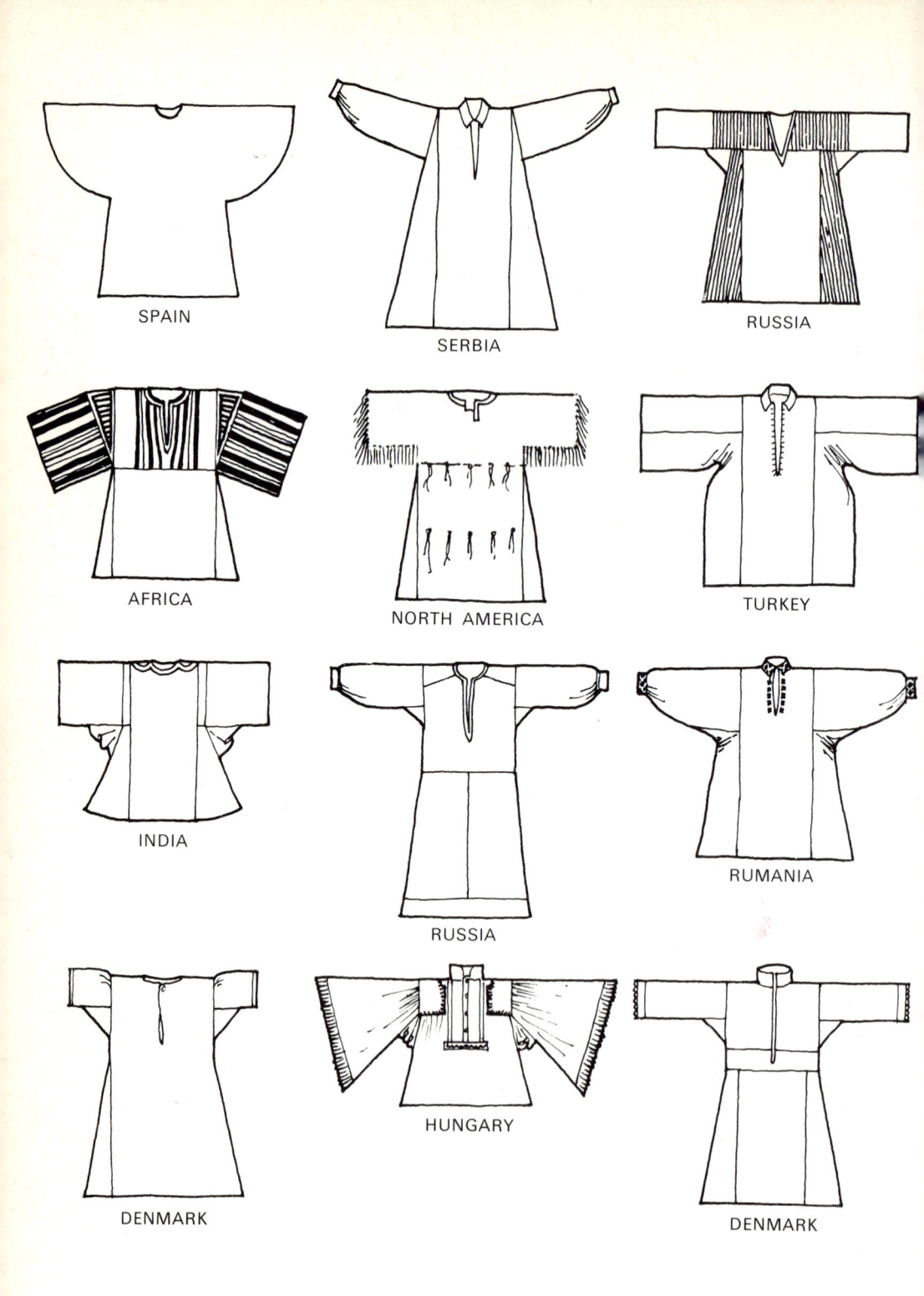

Figure 35. Types of tunic and coat.

THE ANORAK

'Anore' is Eskimo for 'wind', which tells us something about the demands made on this garment. The anorak fits so tightly round the waist, at the wrists and round the opening of the hood, that the wind cannot force its way in.

Figure 36. A sealer wearing a sealskin kayak garment. *Photograph: Jette Bang, 1956. The Arctic Institute, Charlottenlund, Denmark.*

Two races settled in Greenland; first the Eskimos from North America and subsequently, under the leadership of Eric the Red, the Norsemen from Iceland. Eric the Red arrived on this, the biggest island in the world, in 982 and it was he who christened it Greenland.

The Norsemen settled in the south western part of the country and founded Østerbygden and Vesterbygden, now Julianehåb and Godthåb respectively. They tried to introduce their European way

Figure 37. Two children, Angmagssalik, Greenland. *Photograph: Jette Bang. The Arctic Institute, Charlottenlund, Denmark.*

of life to these new and entirely different surroundings. They lived by farming but climatic changes reversed their fortune, shortening their time in Greenland. After about 500 years no more Norsemen were left there.

The Eskimos who migrated from North America to Greenland adapted much more easily to the new conditions. They lived as hunters and fishermen and developed ideal methods of sealing and whaling, and ideal types of dwellings and clothes. Amongst the Eskimo skin clothes we find the precursors of the anorak.

The common sealskin garment, which is still used today, consists of an outer and inner fur whose hairy sides face each other. The air between the two layers has an insulating effect which enables the sealer to lie on the ice for hours, awaiting the appearance of the seal in the breathing hole.

In the Arctic regions the Eskimos used the skin of seals, bears, dogs, reindeer, birds and fish. These skins were used to fulfil particular occupational and climatic requirements and their size and shape was fully exploited. At times the Eskimos' waterproof clothes were made of thin, narrow casings, stitched together to make practical garments. They also made use of the so-called 'water skins', that is, sealskins which were depilated by soaking in urine.

Amongst other things 'water skins' were used for making a special garment worn by whalers when hunting. This garment looks like a bunting with sleeves and legs, and the whaler steps into it through a hole in front. The garment is then inflated a little and laced up tightly. When the hood is also laced up tightly, the whaler can venture out into the water to approach the whale. The garment keeps him warm and when he glides into the water it keeps him afloat for a while. A specimen of this type of garment, no longer much used, can be seen at the Danish National Museum in Copenhagen.

Another characteristic skin garment is the kayak anorak which is also made of water skin. When the bottom edge of the kayak anorak is laced up tightly round the opening of the kayak, the experienced sealer can roll the light boat in the water without letting water into it.

It was the man's job to procure food and skin. Treating the skins, cutting them out and making them into clothes were tasks for the woman. We know only little about the cutting out process but it is obvious that it is based on a highly developed, practical feeling for shape combined with a keen eye.

The shapes of Eskimo skin clothes are adapted to the requirements of people living in Arctic regions. The garments have sleeves attached at right angles which, combined with the length of the hood (see page 93), makes the garment broad across the chest and shoulders and under the arms, providing freedom of movement, for example to throw a harpoon. This width also makes

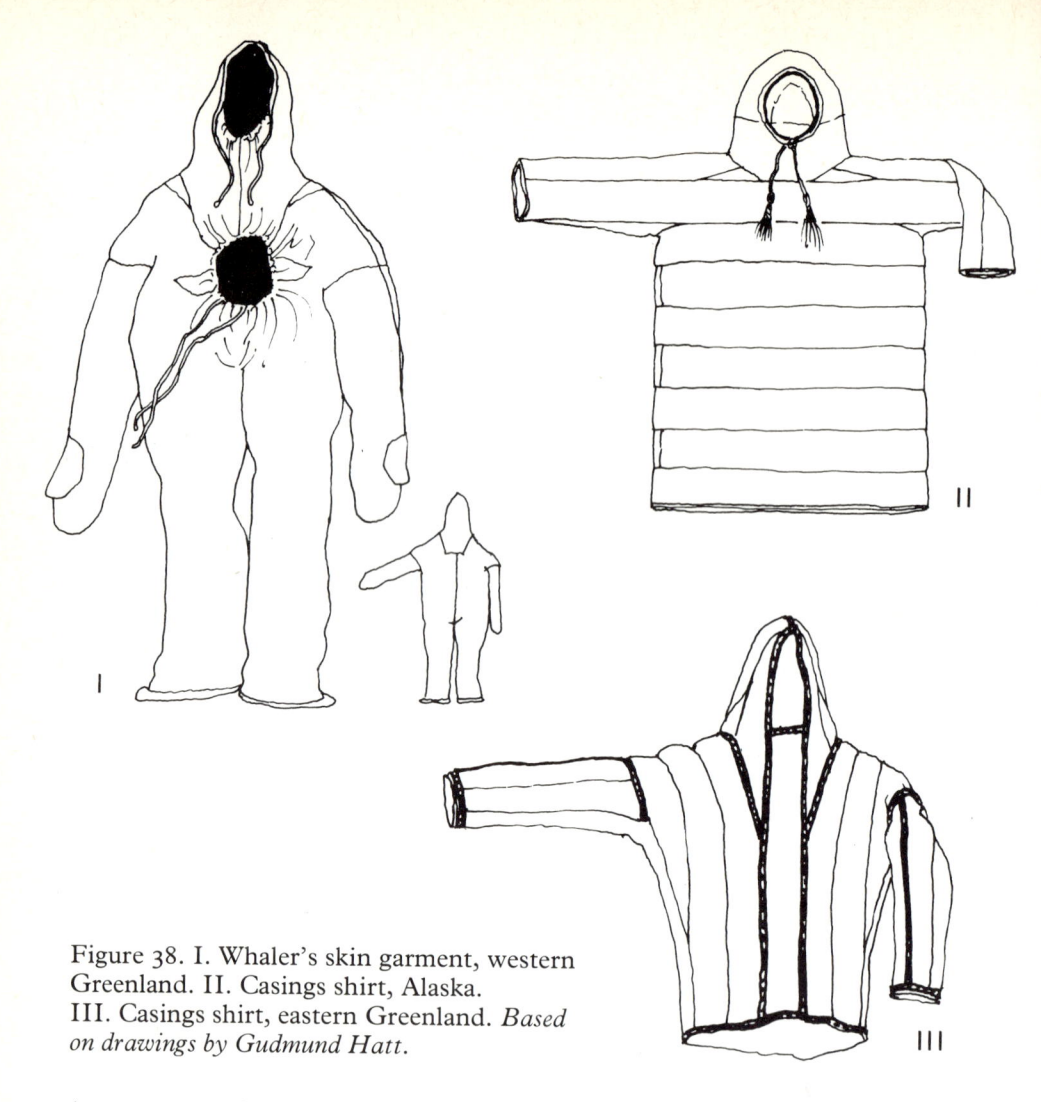

Figure 38. I. Whaler's skin garment, western Greenland. II. Casings shirt, Alaska.
III. Casings shirt, eastern Greenland. *Based on drawings by Gudmund Hatt.*

it easy to put the naked arms into the skin garment, as the Eskimos used to do.

It is obvious that, although a formalisation of the shape took place when the anorak was transferred from skin to woven material, the proportions and the position of the hood have been retained. The characteristic sewing technique used by the Greenlanders for sewing on the hood is reminiscent of their way of using skin.

Around the opening of the hood, at the cuffs and bottom edge the skin garment was close-fitting and bordered with narrow strips of skin cut on the bias so as to increase the wearability of the garment. These borders remain in the festive anorak as decorative trimmings.

If we look at the modernised anorak with its width and length, and the openings in the actual outline of the shape for zips and fastenings, we find that a radical change has taken place compared with the traditional Eskimo anorak.

Today, however, more and more young Greenlanders wear the traditional anorak in order to emphasise their distinctive cultural identity.

Figure 39. Eskimo man's skin anorak, western Greenland. The body consists of two skins. The front one reaches up across the shoulders and well down the back, while the back one reaches up to form the greater part of the hood. At the top of the hood a gusset is inserted. This type of hood is probably one of the precursors of the Greenland anorak hood. *Based on drawings by Gudmund Hatt.*

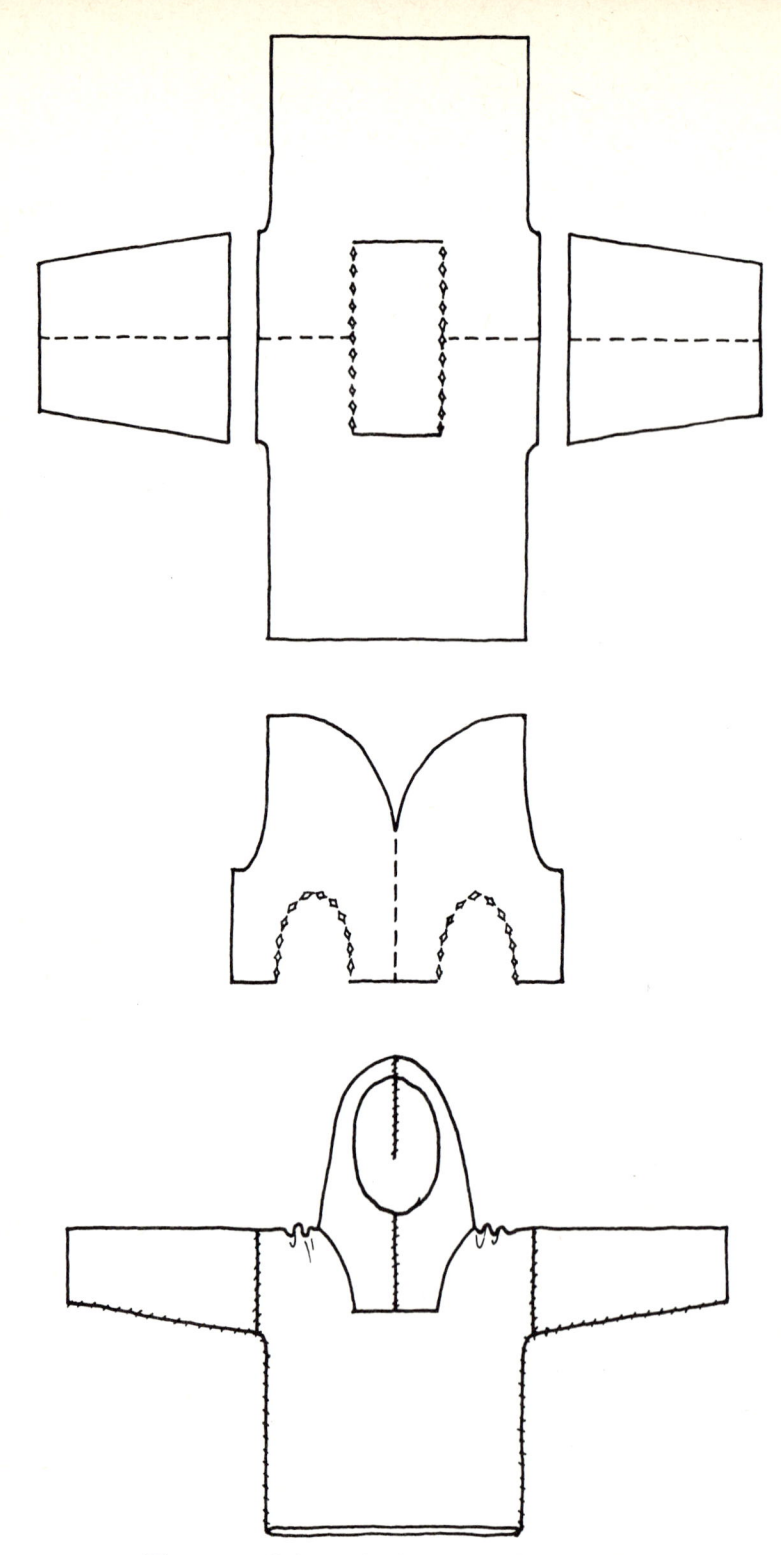

Figure 40. Schematic drawings of the anorak.

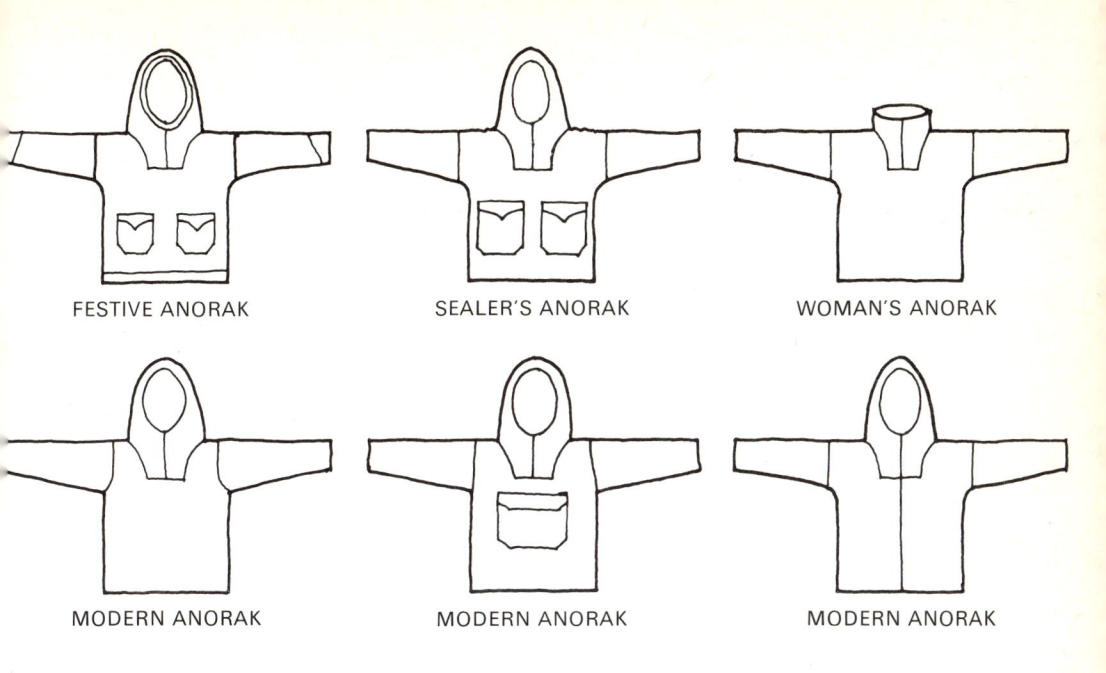

| FESTIVE ANORAK | SEALER'S ANORAK | WOMAN'S ANORAK |
| MODERN ANORAK | MODERN ANORAK | MODERN ANORAK |

Figure 41. Anorak types.

THE CAFTAN

Unlike the garments described so far the caftan is open in front. It has a certain width created by means of gussets inserted in front and at the sides.

There are several types of caftans. One version is worn in Central and East Asia by both men and women, where it is so long that it hides the trousers. Waistcoats and jerseys are worn on top of or under the caftan. The number of layers indicates social status.

Henny Harald Hansen in particular has dealt with Asian types of clothing. In *Man makes clothes—clothes make the man* she compares the geographical distribution of the caftan with the silk route from China to Europe. She relates how the caravans travelled through deserts and across vertiginous mountain passes carrying the miraculous silk fabric, whose origin remained a secret in Europe up to the fourth century A.D. when two monks brought some silk moth eggs to Constantinople after a journey deep into Central Asia. Subsequently the production of silk started in Europe and it might have been expected that the Asian trouser suit and caftan would have been imported to Europe at the same time. However it was only during the Renaissance that the caftan, the precursor of our common, indispensable coat, was adopted into our culture.

Figure 42. Asian girls in caftans. *Photograph: China Reconstructs.*

THE KIMONO

The kimono is related to the caftan, but is made of rectangular lengths of material. It is the traditional Japanese costume which has been worn by both men and women for centuries. According to the season the kimono is worn singly or several are worn on top of each other.

The very wide sleeves of the kimono are often sewn so that they form a bag at the bottom which can be used for carrying small articles.

The kimono is wrapped smoothly round the body, the man's being held together with a narrow belt, the woman's with a very broad one, called an obi.

The long kimono worn by the woman was originally puffed up around a belt on top of which the obi was tied, often with a very complex knot or bow at the back, which gave the woman a soft and flower-like silhouette.

Festive and ceremonial kimonos are made of heavy silk, while everyday ones are made of cotton. The material is chosen according to how the kimono is to be decorated—whether it is to be

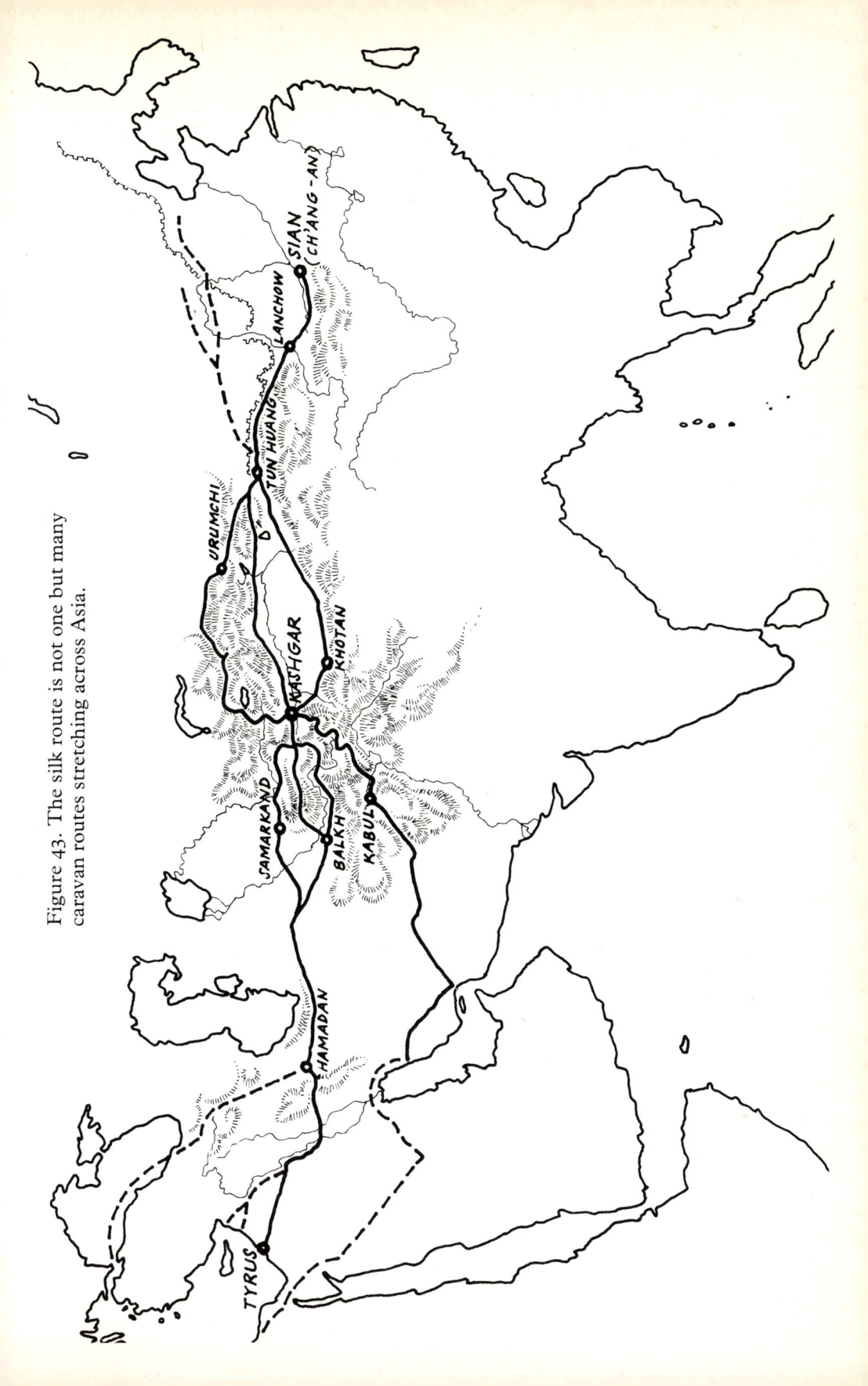

Figure 43. The silk route is not one but many caravan routes stretching across Asia.

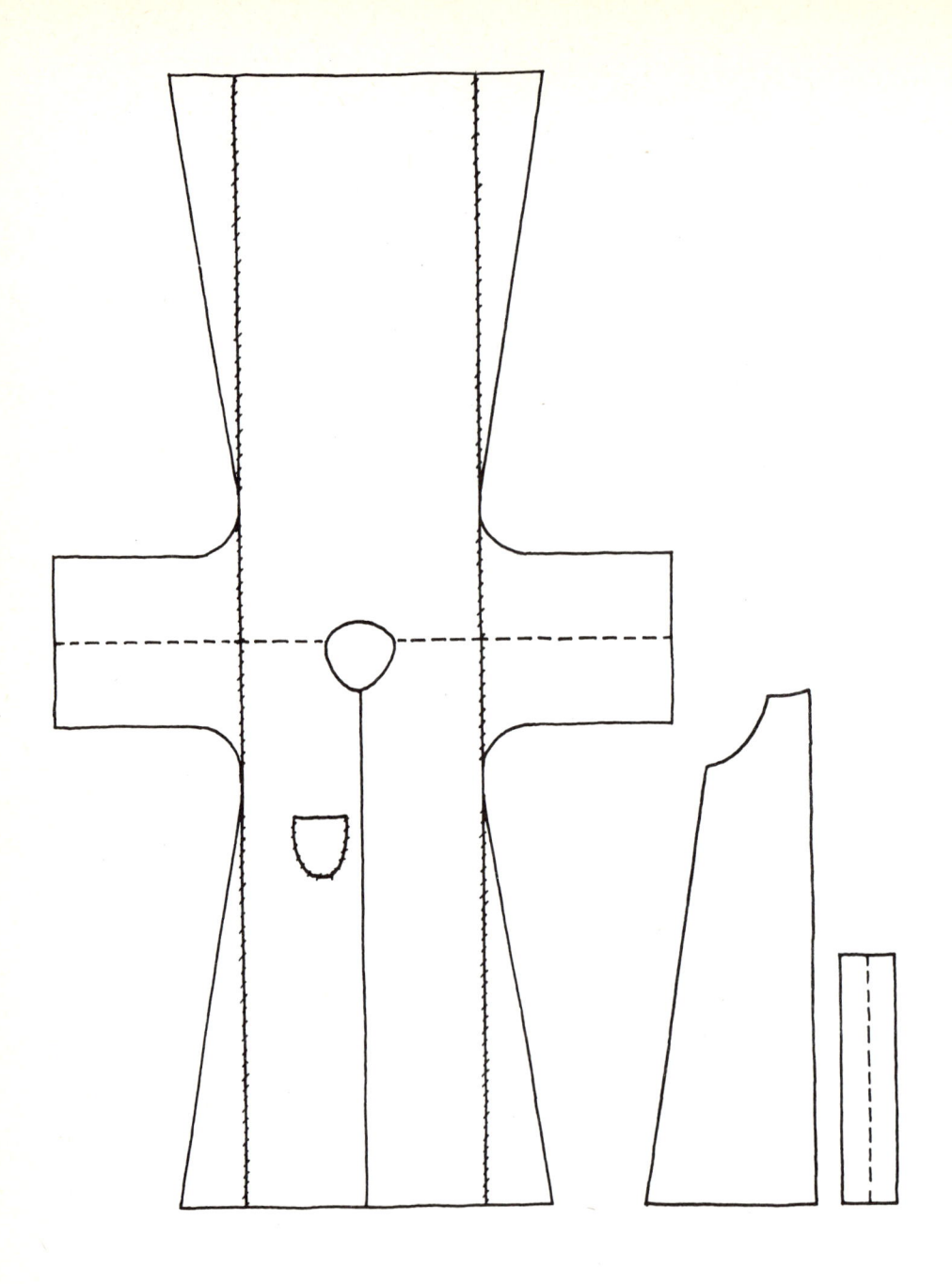

Figure 44. Schematic drawing of the caftan.

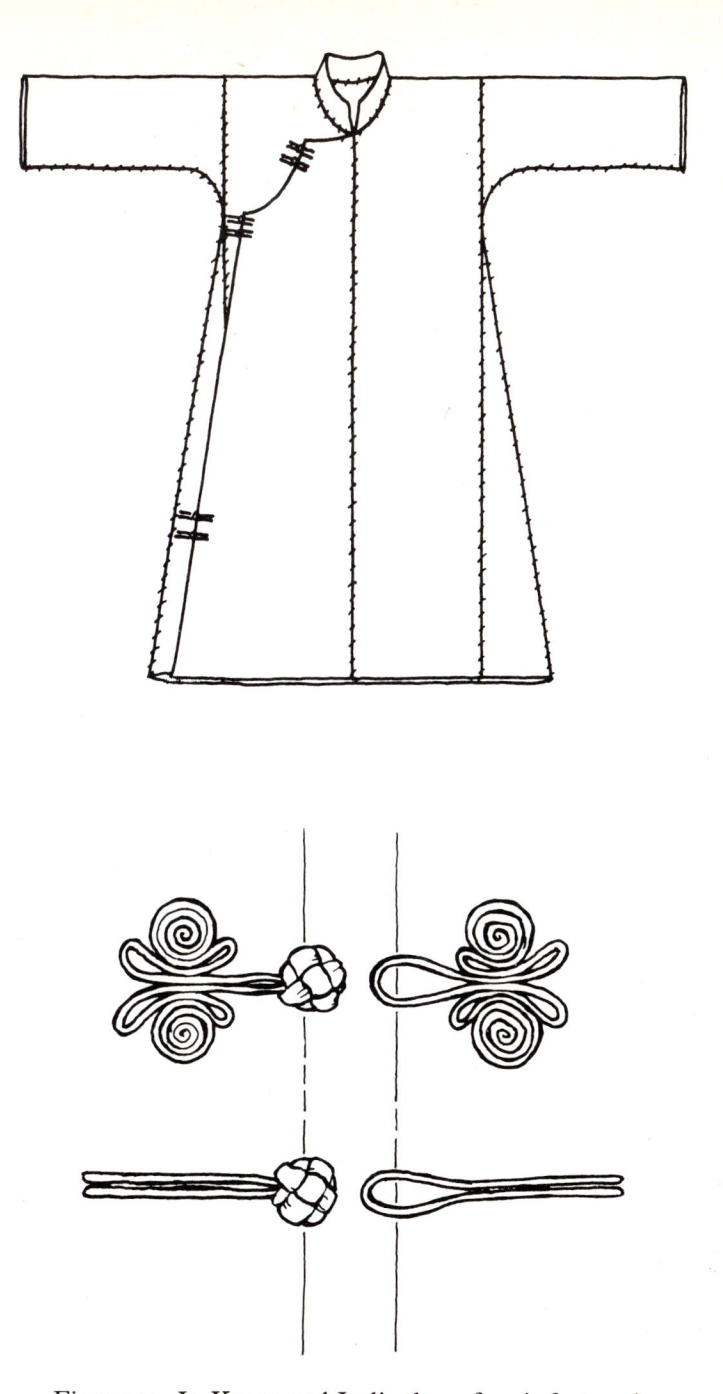

Figure 45. In Korea and India the caftan is fastened with tie-strings, while in Mongolia and China it is fastened with toggles and loops. The idea of piercing the material to create a buttonhole was not general in any of these countries.

TIBET

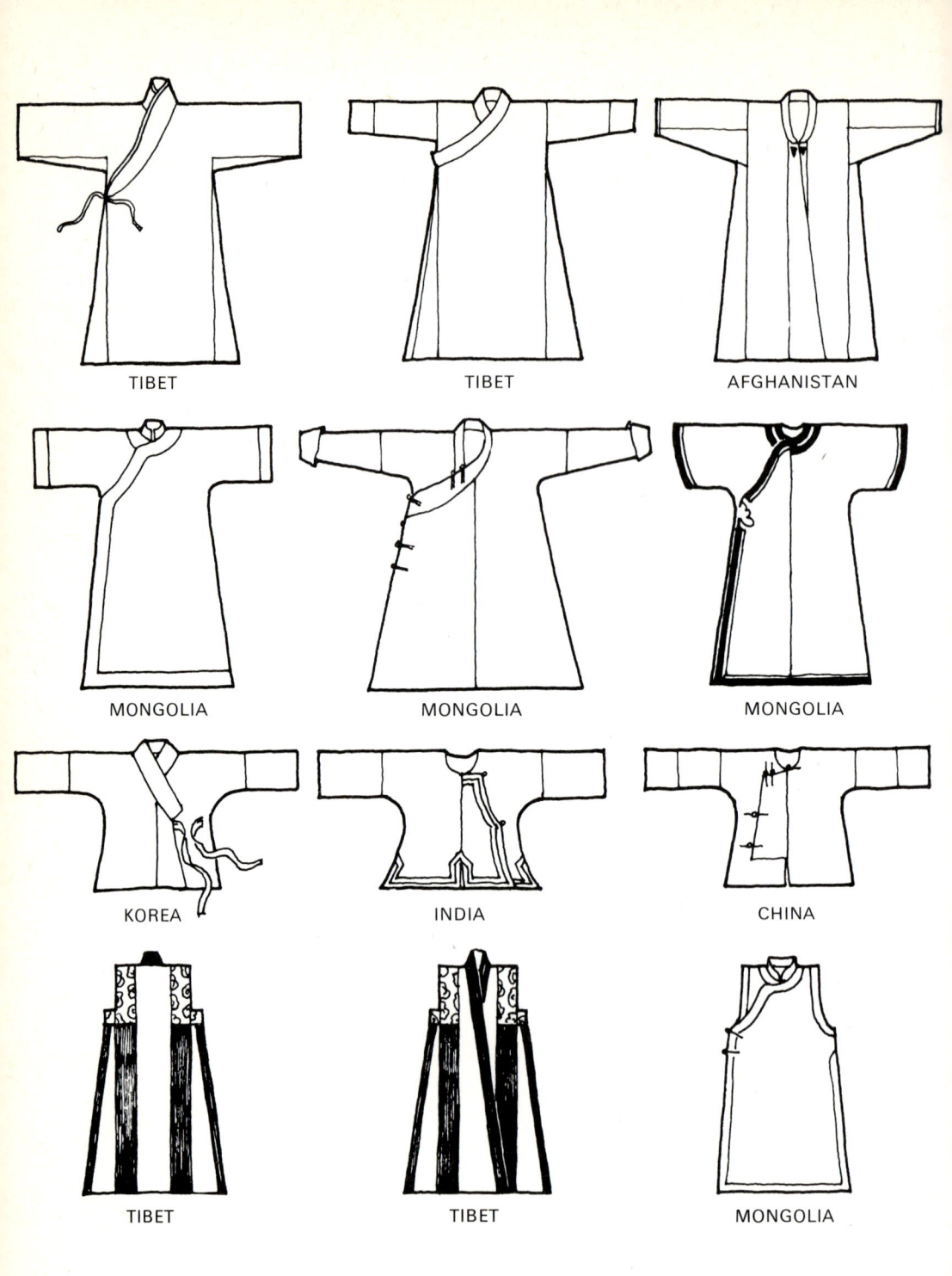

TIBET

AFGHANISTAN

MONGOLIA

MONGOLIA

MONGOLIA

KOREA

INDIA

CHINA

TIBET

TIBET

MONGOLIA

Figure 46. Caftan types.

EGYPT   EGYPT   TURKEY

Figure 47. Caftan types continued.

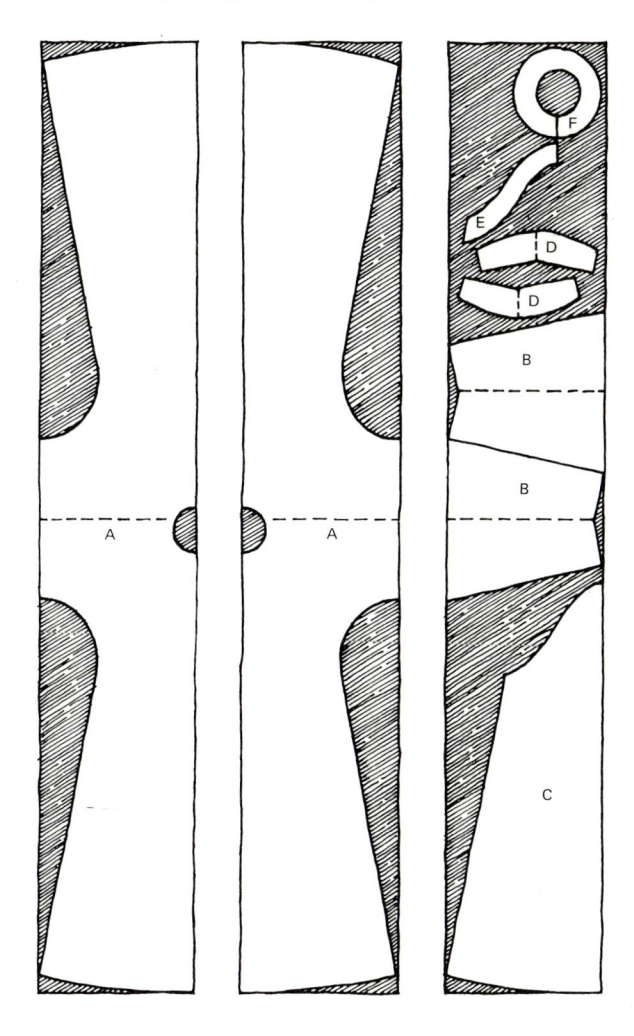

Figure 48. Chinese caftan.

55

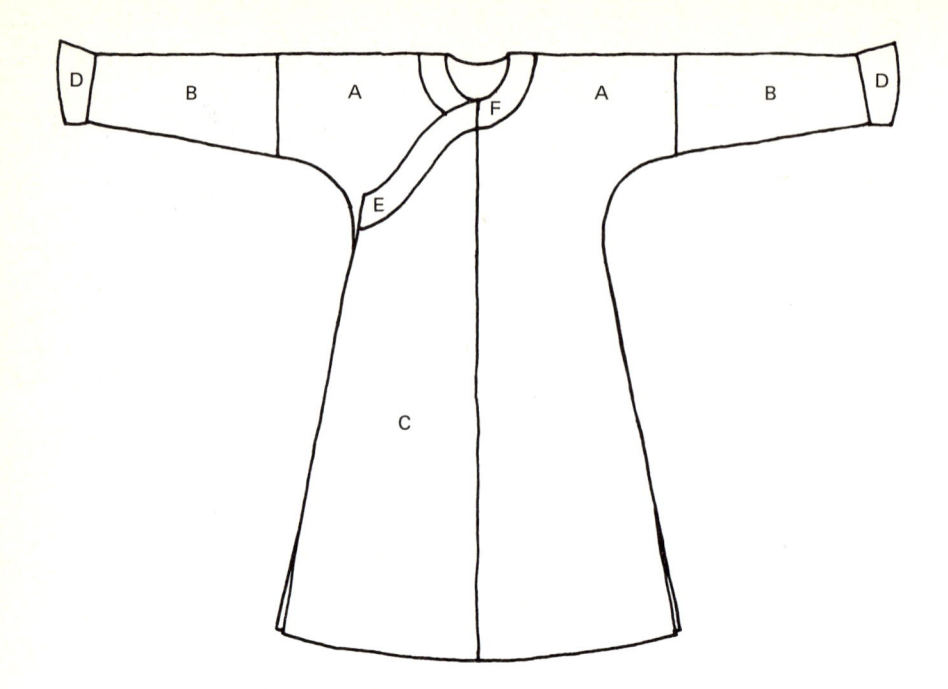

Figure 49. Chinese caftan continued.

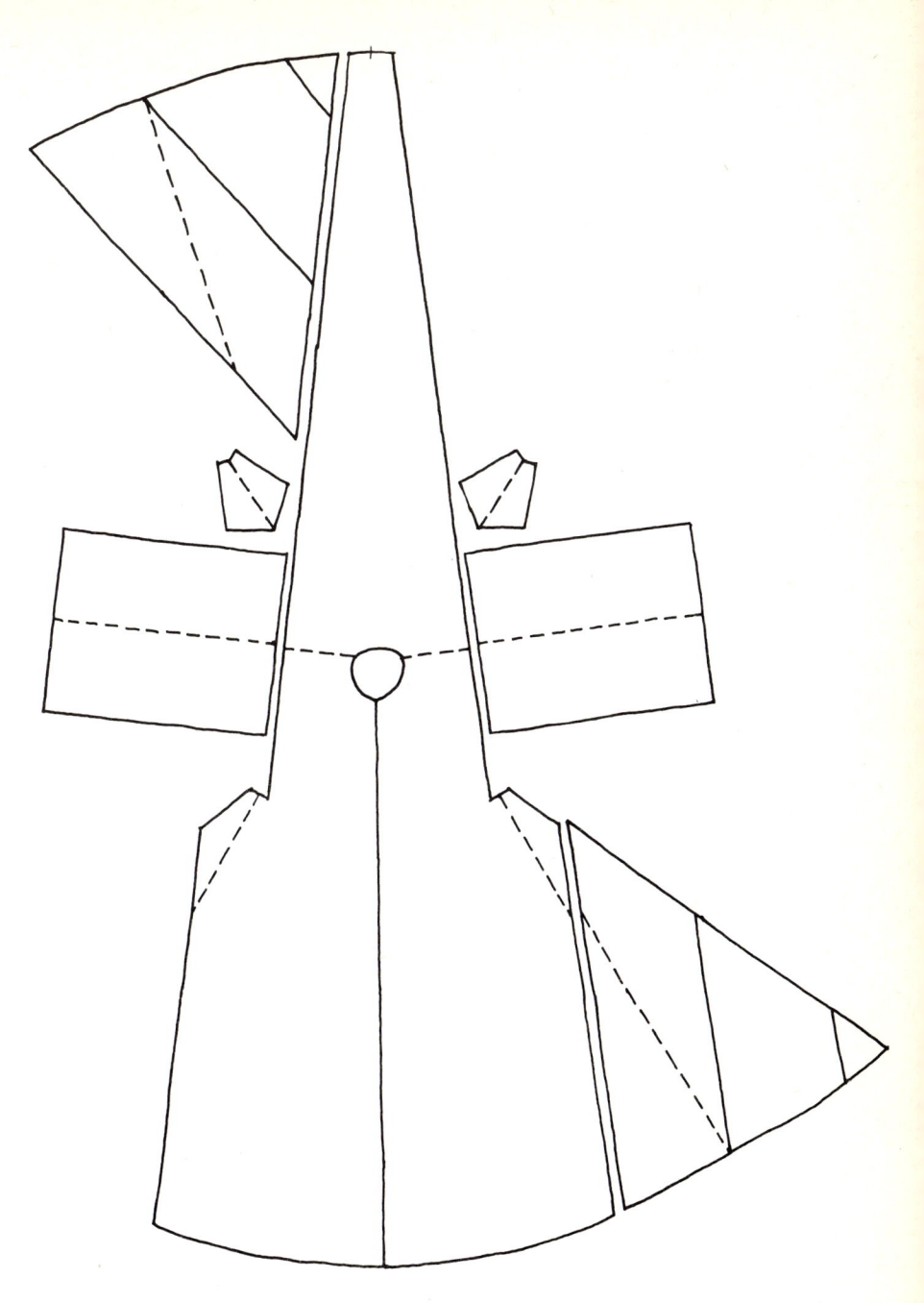

Figure 50. Egyptian caftan type. Note the slanting shoulder line (see also the section on waistcoats).

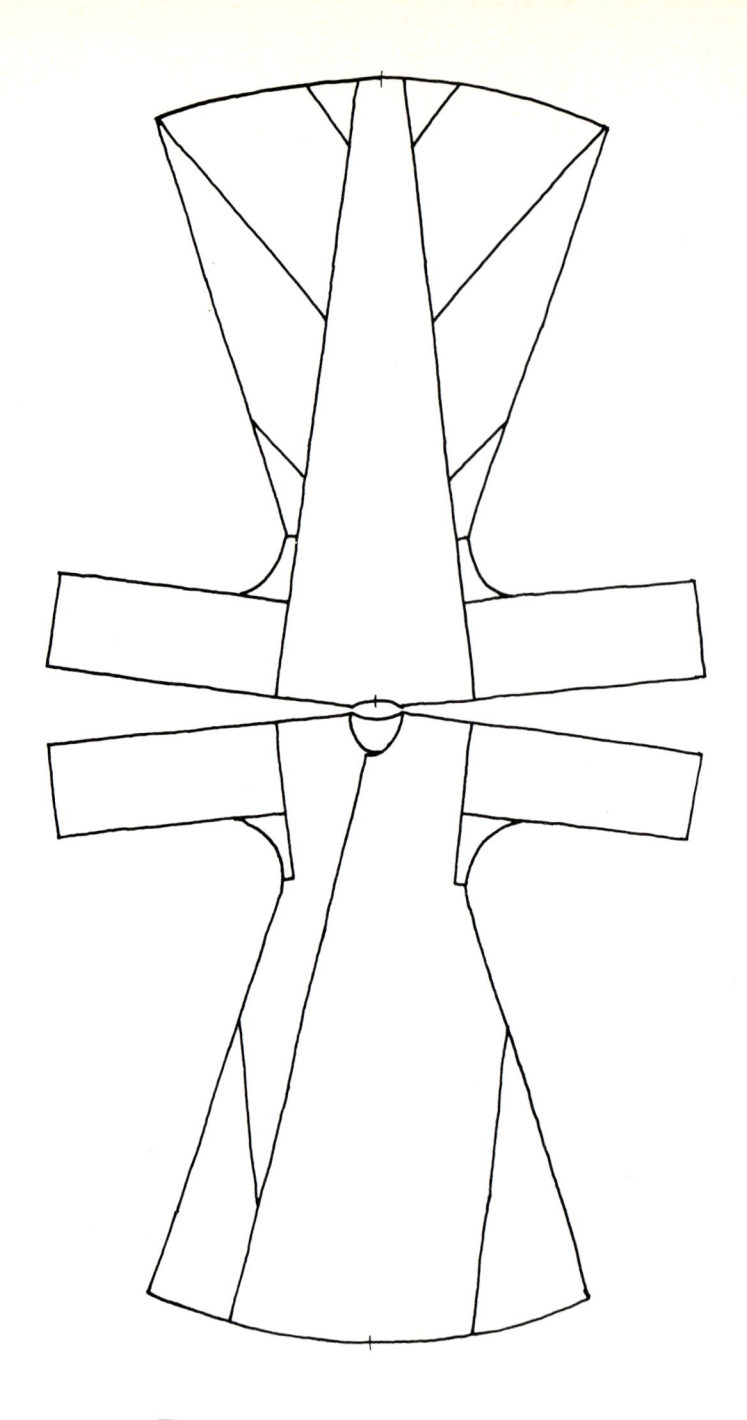

Figure 51. Egyptian caftan continued.

embroidered, decorated with appliqué work, painted, or decorated with a special Japanese template colour-technique, the principle of which is similar to that of batik.

Decoration, materials and colours were determined by the prevailing fashion as well as by the person's social and marital status but the fashioning of the kimono has always followed a fixed scheme. Therefore, before sewing a new kimono the dyer is consulted to make arrangements about motifs and colours.

Figure 52.

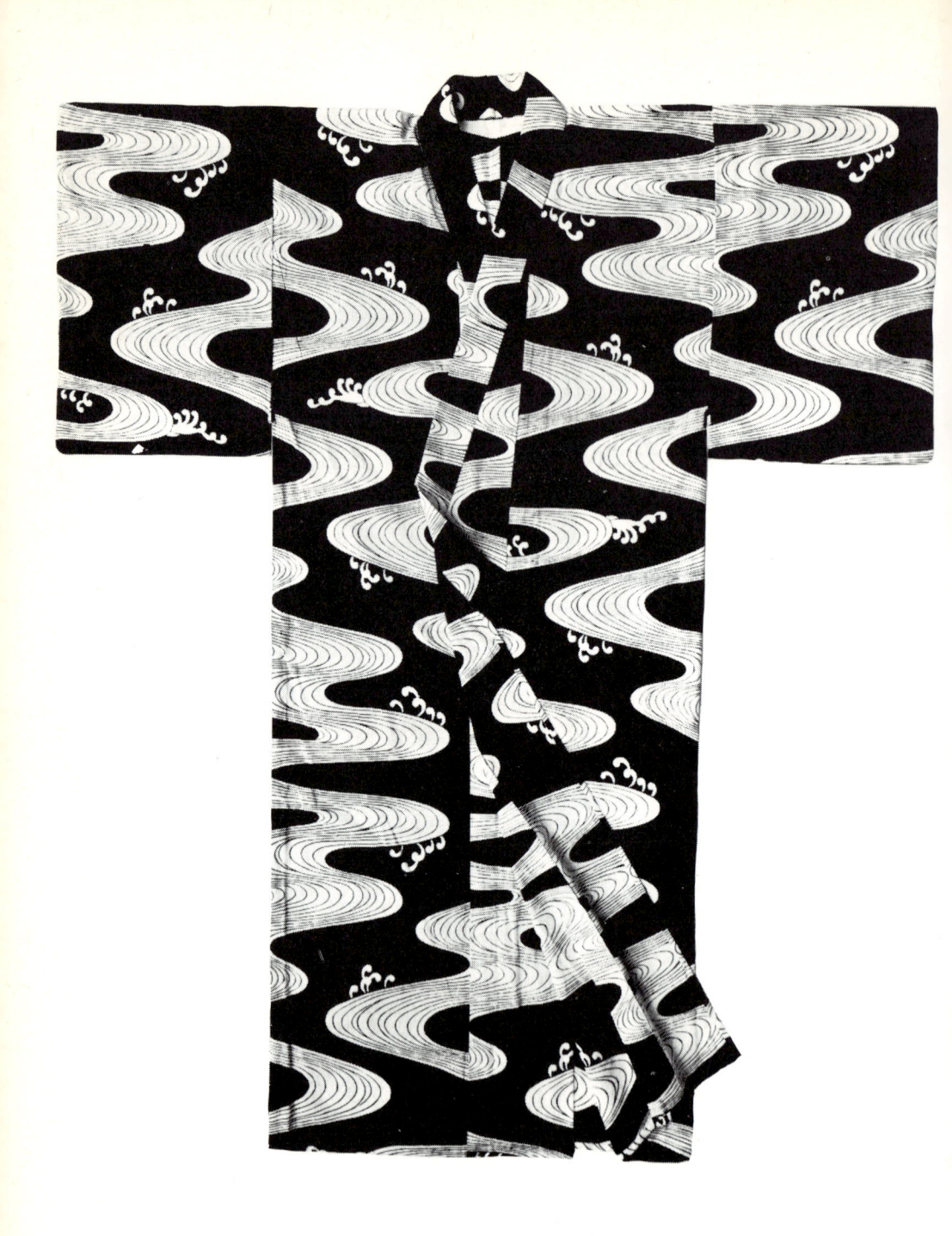

Figure 53. Cotton summer kimono with a white wave motif on an indigo ground. *Photograph from: Japanese Articles for Everyday Use. The kimono is the property of Else Stephensen.*

Figure 54.

The same width of material is used for all sizes. If a smaller size is required the turnings at the sides and at the centre back are simply made wider. The stitching together of the lengths of material is so simple that it is common to unstitch the seams before washing and ironing a fine kimono.

Asymmetrical plant ornaments, such as bamboo and flowering cherry twigs, are typical motifs to be found on the traditional kimono. Often the symbols used are incomprehensible to a Westerner. Originally the colours of the kimono were determined by traditions or rules. Servants and coolies wore blue clothes. Brown and black were considered particularly becoming for younger men, and even today the everyday summer kimono is blue or brownish.

A marriage ritual still exists which prescribes a change of colour. The bride wears three kimonos—two white ones on top and a red one underneath. In the course of the ceremony she takes off the two white ones, leaving only the red one which symbolises happiness. The red kimono was at one time recommended for everyday wear as the intensity of the colour gave the pale skin on the face a seductive, blushing glow which suggested the flowers of the Japanese flowering cherry.

The characteristic socks fashioned to the natural shape of the foot are still worn indoors. Together with the light kimono they harmonise well with the simple furniture of Japanese houses and with the natural materials that characterise the original Japanese milieu.

Figure 55.

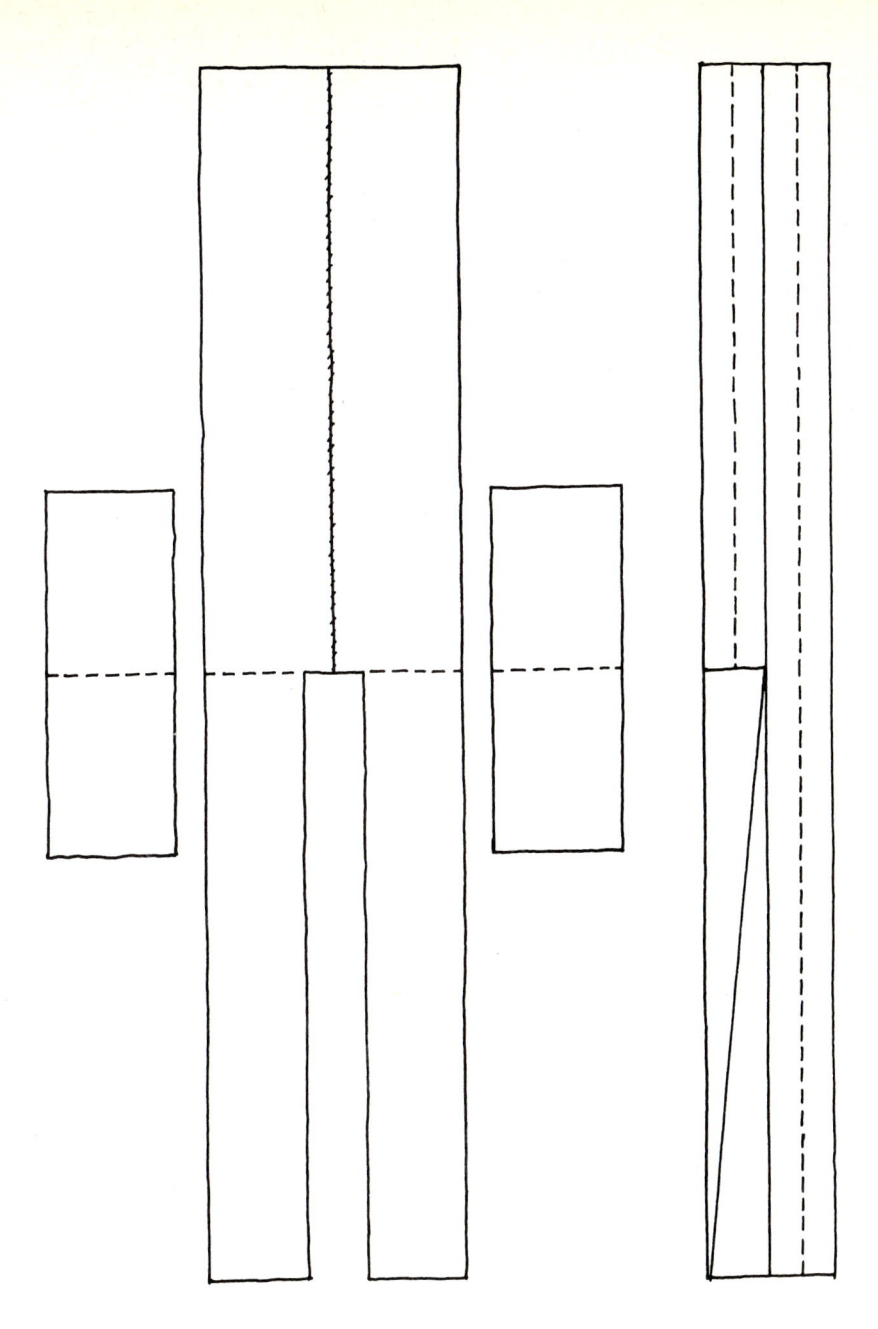

Figure 56. Schematic drawing of the kimono.

JACKET

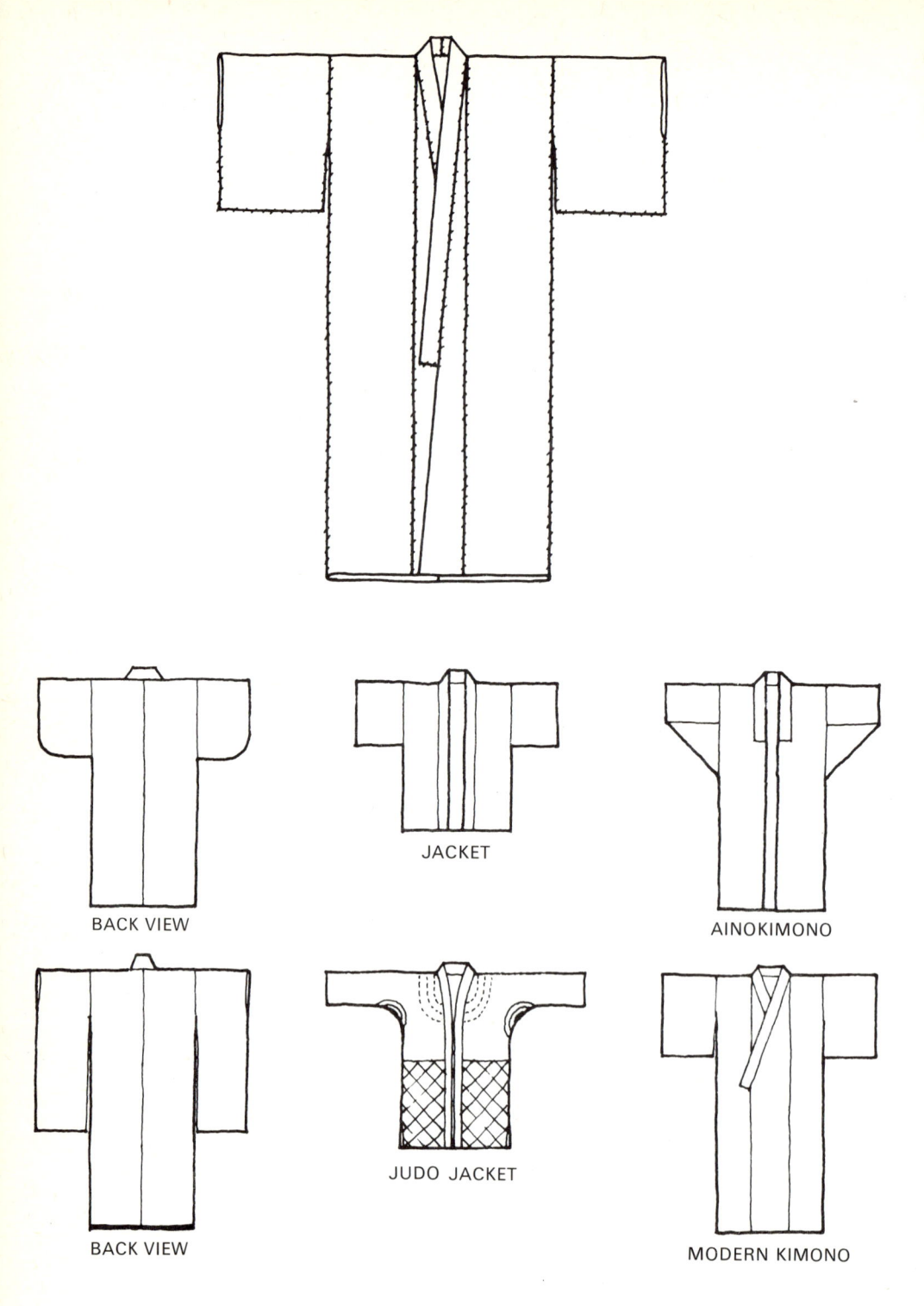

BACK VIEW

AINOKIMONO

JUDO JACKET

BACK VIEW

MODERN KIMONO

Figure 57. Kimono types.

THE WAISTCOAT

The waistcoat is comparatively late in origin. It has no sleeves and is generally open in front or at the side. It is found almost everywhere—worn partly to warm the body, but also at times for decorative purposes only.

The waistcoat constitutes an important part of many European national costumes.

We have sketched some examples here to enable the reader to compare the design to that of the garments described above and look at the relationship between them.

If the shoulder line of the waistcoat is slanting, a triangle (gusset) has been removed from the basic shape, making the waistcoat more tight-fitting. Similarly, triangular sections could be removed in many other places, although these principles of fitting are different from those dealt with in this book.

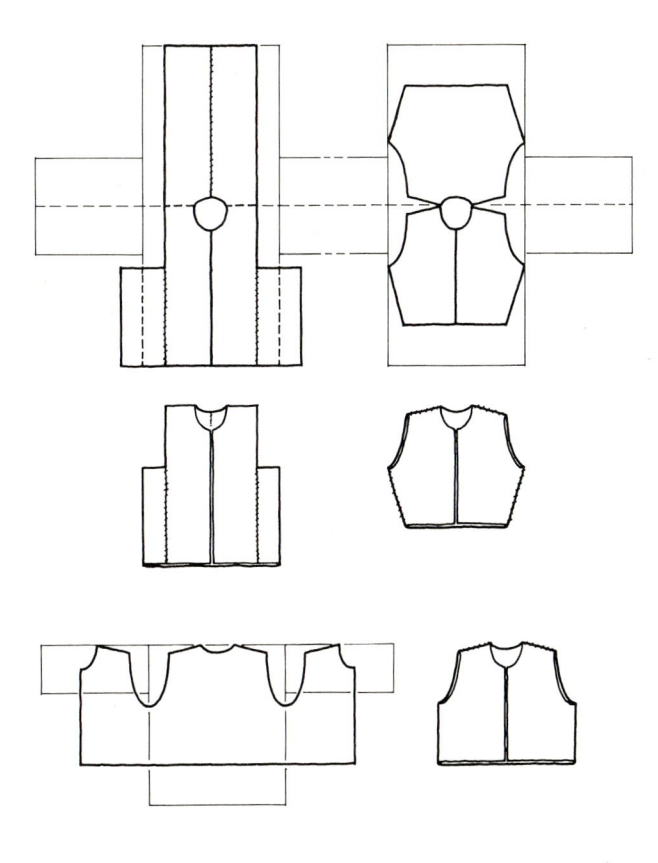

Figure 58. Schematic drawings of waistcoats.

Figure 59. Waistcoat types.

Clothes and their function

Now that a number of forms of clothing have been described from the point of view of their origin, and the unstitched and sewn garments have been dealt with in schematic drawings, it is logical that we should attempt to sum up the reasons for the shape of these clothes.

The decoration of clothes is not the subject of this book although it does influence their structure. A richly decorated piece of material does not invite a complicated pattern which would spoil the ornamental effect of the fabric. However, clothes with a simple cut, such as the kanga and the poncho, encourage the use of decorative patterns.

The influence of design on the shape of the garment increases with the symbolic importance of the costume and in many ceremonial garments the cultic precepts are so strong that they over-shadow practical considerations completely; this can be observed in medicine men's garments, for example, or in the often useless scraps of clothes amongst the Inca finds.

These simple kinds of clothes are not particularly dependent on social factors and it is the choice of colours and fabrics which indicates social status. Examples of this are the kimono, the caftan, or the tunic type, all of which have been worn by both slaves and emperors. Among the upper classes in most societies, however, we do find a number of superfluous articles of clothing which indicate the status of the wearer. A wealth of different types of clothing exist which exclude physical work, thereby showing that the wearer does not occupy himself with that kind of thing. (Just think of the royal garments from the Baroque period).

Taste and aesthetics have a marked influence on the form of the garment. As an example we can mention the Greek peplus which is a stylistic expression on a par with the architecture and sculpture of antiquity.

The philosophy of different cultures is also reflected in the clothes. The kanga could not have been created or worn everywhere. Traditions, habits, and ways of life also play a major role. The hang in the simple Japanese kimono is in accordance with the ideal of a gliding gait, a certain carriage and a certain sitting posture.

Climate, landscape and occupation have also affected the fashioning of clothes. During the Bronze Age, when agriculture replaced hunting as a means of subsistence, clothes were no longer restricted by the possibilities offered by animal skin. With the introduction of weaving it became possible, for example, to fashion large, wide skirts even though the outline of the skin can still be seen, for example in the Bronze Age girl's blouse. The shape of the anorak is conditional on and adapted to the geographical conditions at one and the same time. It protects against wind and weather and it is tight-fitting without ever hampering movement.

These factors are important for the development of the shape of clothes but the availability in a culture of types of materials and tools is quite fundamental.

Before the industrial revolution the manufacture of fabrics was a slow process. The wool had to be cut, cleaned, carded, spun, and perhaps dyed, all by hand, before the actual weaving could begin.

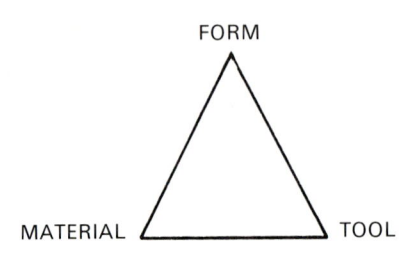

```
            FORM
             /\
            /  \
           /    \
          /      \
MATERIAL /_____\ TOOL
```

Figure 60.

The tool used for the working up of the raw material makes the fabric and defines its form. The width of the material is dependent on the type of loom available. Weaving was time-consuming and it is understandable that people were eager to exploit fully the laboriously woven pieces of material but it is difficult to say whether it is the width of the material which determines the shape of a garment or vice versa. If widths of material broader than the capacity of the loom were needed, several widths were simply stitched together (see figs. 61 and 62).

Apart from economical reasons the advantages for craftsmen of stitching together the selvedges of the widths of material were obvious. These advantages, and, perhaps more important the power of tradition, have determined that garments continued to be made up of quadrangular pieces, even after the introduction of other, more rational types of loom.

The Huldre bog garment, the tubular shape which was woven on a circular loom, can be seen as another example of the close connection between tools, materials and design.

In times of crisis, when the principle of recycling has to be applied, the fashioning of new clothes will often bear the stamp of the shape of the old clothes from which they have been made, (*cf* also the exploitation of the skin for the Bronze Age blouse).

Geographical possibilities of interchange also influence the way of dressing. The caftan is an example of this.

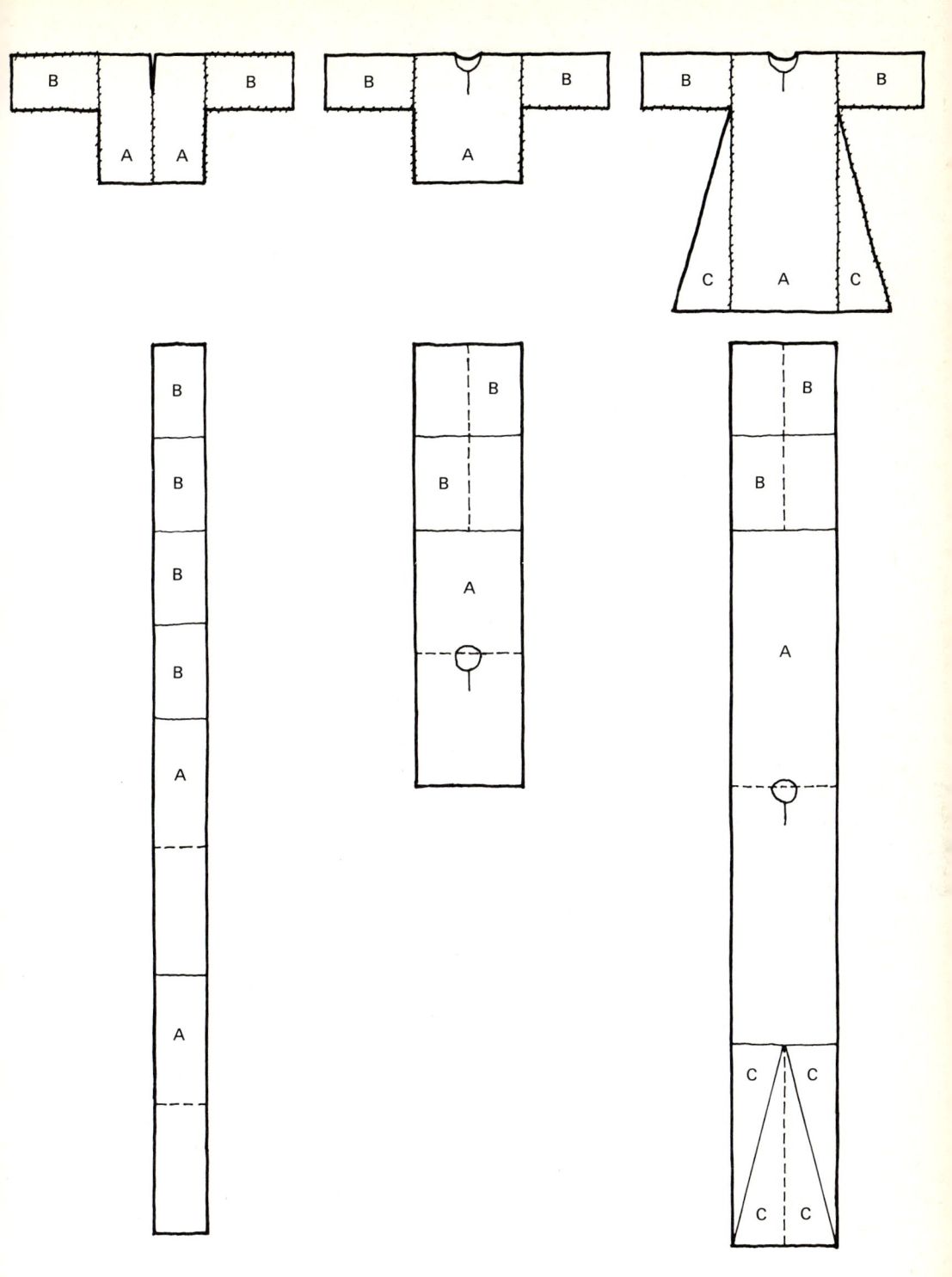

Figure 61. Examples of how the width of the material can be used.

Figure 62. Examples of how the width of the material can be used.

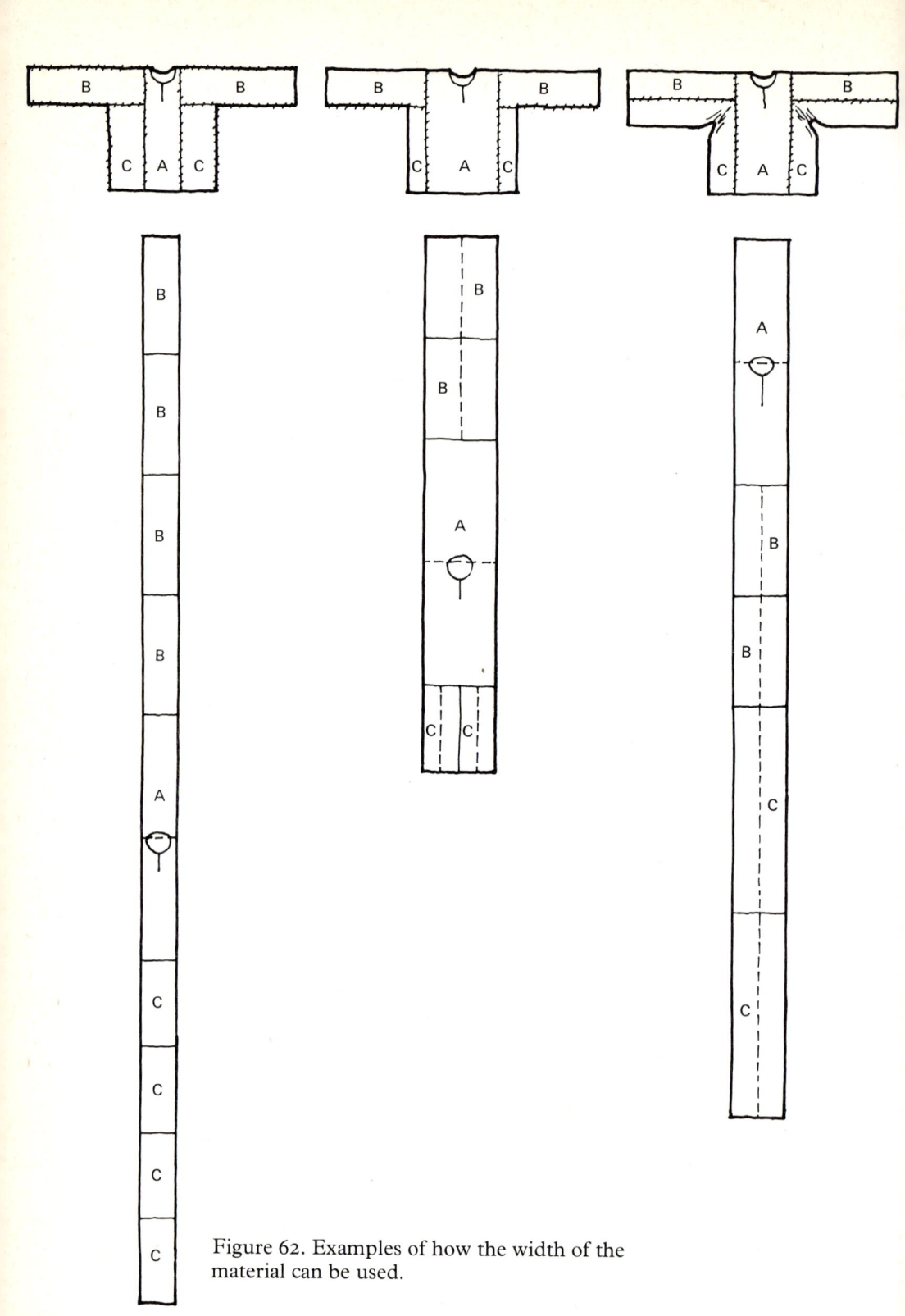

```
            EXPRESSION
               /\
              /  \
             /    \
            /      \
           /        \
     MAN  /_____\  CLOTHES
```

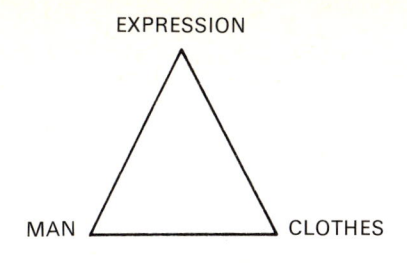

Figure 63.

All these original types of garments can be regarded as being cultural expressions which tell us something about the time, the place and the way of life which influenced their design. But the interrelations can be difficult to unravel and an attempt at a synthesis is bound to be a simplification. Therefore, by way of conclusion we will look at some critical and independent evaluations which will give a more varied picture of the complexity of the development of forms of garments.

The function of the basic shape

The individual body is the shape used as a basis for the manufacturing of personal clothes (see page 13).

Before starting to make clothes it is helpful to distinguish between three categories: wide, loose and tight-fitting clothes. Some clothes are worn next to the body, some are worn as top garments, and so on. It is practical, therefore, to draw three versions of the basic shape: a tight-fitting one, a loose one and a wide one. We would suggest that the first project should be to sew a blouse of thin material, the purpose being to test how tight-fitting the basic shape can be drawn. The three basic shapes are then drawn up according to this test (see opposite).

Two things are crucial to the functional possibilities of the clothes you plan to make; which of the three basic shapes is chosen as the basis for a particular garment, and what kind of material is chosen for the design.

If you wish to make a coat based on the principle of the caftan it can be loose and made in cotton, or it can be very wide, made in wool, and used as a winter coat.

You can therefore begin by asking what the coat is to be used for—and what demands are going to be made on it. According to this, and to the relevant measurements, the basic shape and the material are chosen. Not all combinations are equally practicable. The tunic principle, for example, can only be used for a tight-fitting blouse without arm gussets if it is made of a comparatively thin and soft material. If you want to make a woollen waistcoat, which must be warm and big enough to be worn on top of a thick sweater, you have to choose a basic shape larger than the one required for a silk waistcoat meant to be worn for decorative purposes on top of a thin blouse.

As it will appear these considerations are questions of need, judgement and assessment rather than calculation.

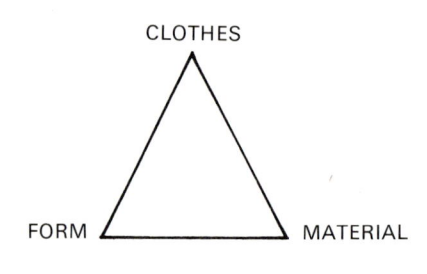

Figure 64.

Drawing the basic shape

THE FOLDED PARTS OF THE BASIC SHAPE

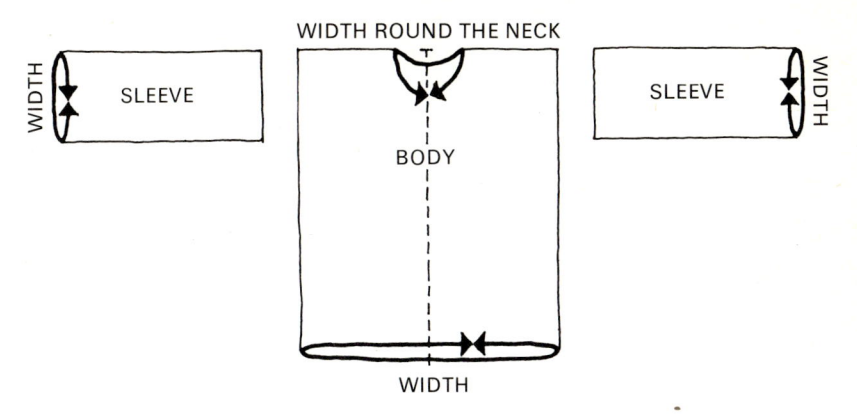

THE UNFOLDED PARTS OF THE BASIC SHAPE

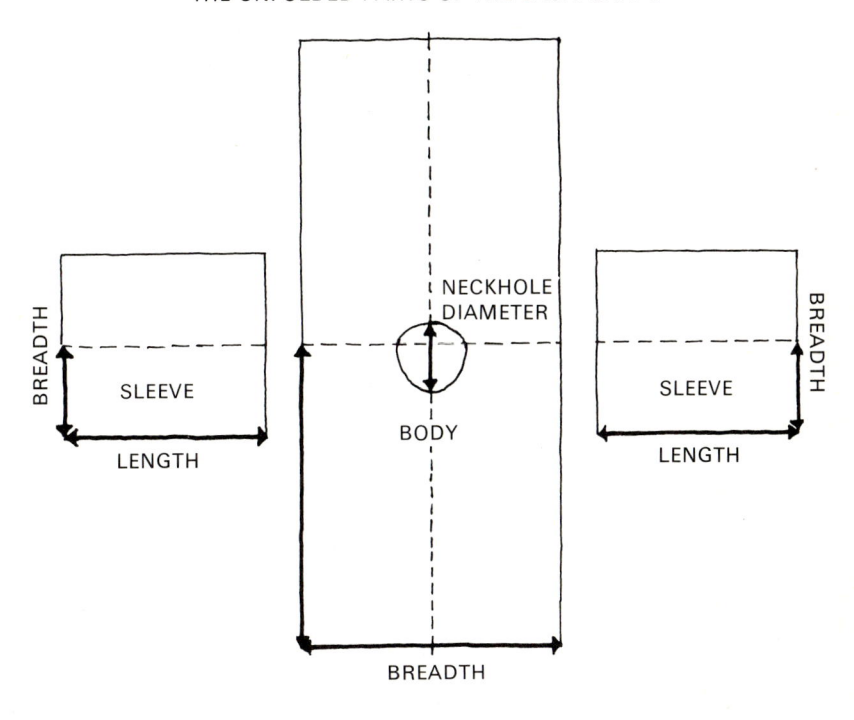

Figure 65.

BASIC BODY MEASUREMENTS

In the section below is a description of how to measure the body (see also page 17). Two people are needed in order for the measurements to be exact. The measurements are noted down in the fig. on page 112. See also figs. 77 and 78.

The width of the body is measured round the broadest part of the chest. Women with a big chest measurement should measure the width of the body comparatively tightly so that the basic shape is not too wide compared to the other parts of the body.

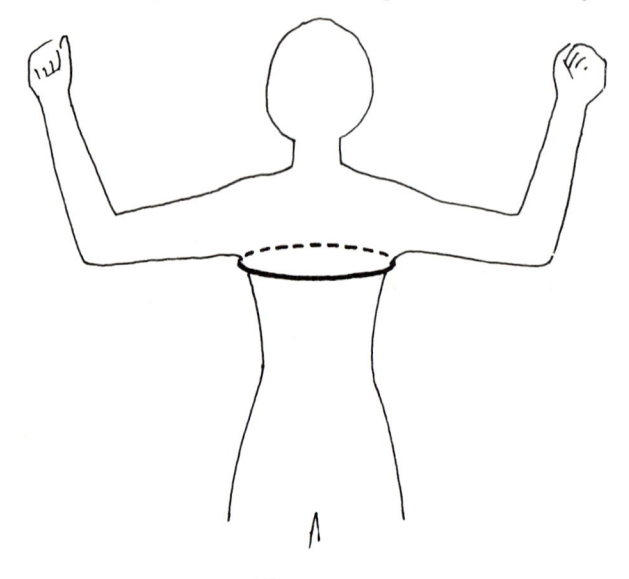

Figure 66.

WIDTH OF THE BODY + EXTRA WIDTH ⟶ BODY WIDTH

$$\frac{\text{WIDTH}}{2} \longrightarrow \text{BREADTH}$$

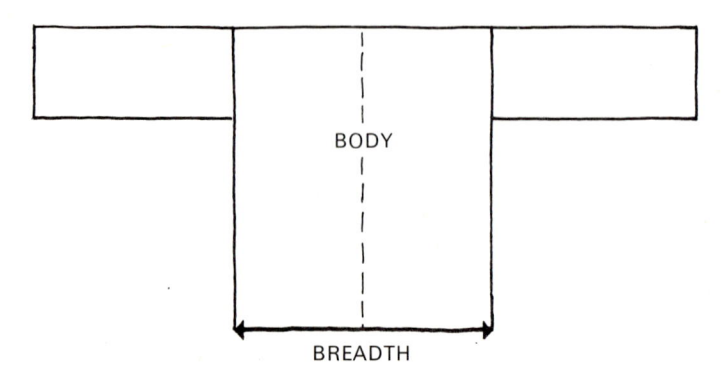

Figure 67.

The width of the arm is measured round the tightened muscle of the upper arm or round the broadest part.

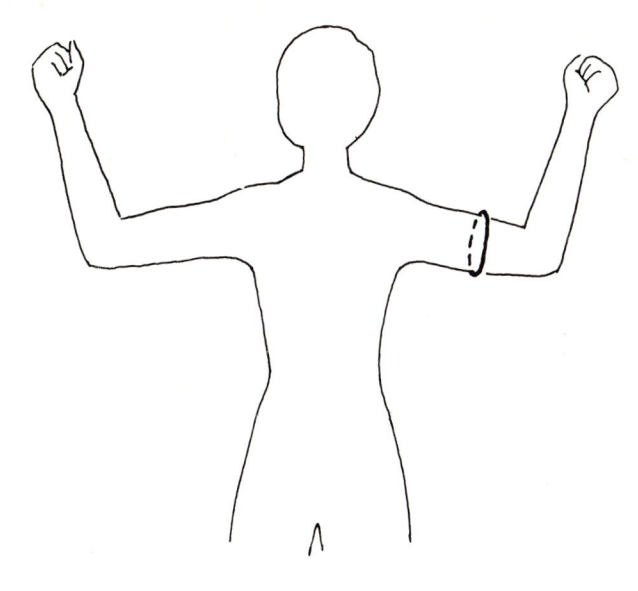

Figure 68.

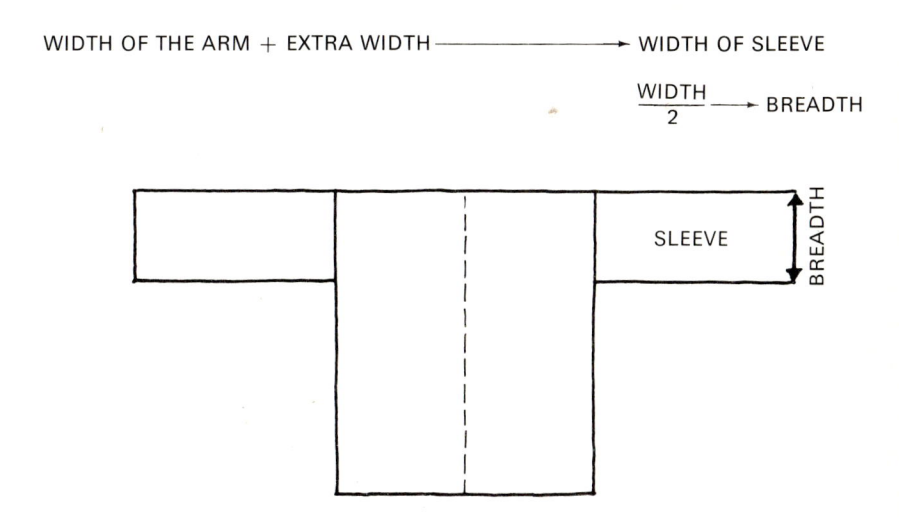

WIDTH OF THE ARM + EXTRA WIDTH ⟶ WIDTH OF SLEEVE

$$\frac{\text{WIDTH}}{2} \rightarrow \text{BREADTH}$$

Figure 69.

The length is measured from the shoulder to the hips. If the garment is to cover the hips, check whether this is practicable. In many cases it may be necessary to bias cut the sides or to make a slit (fig. 92).

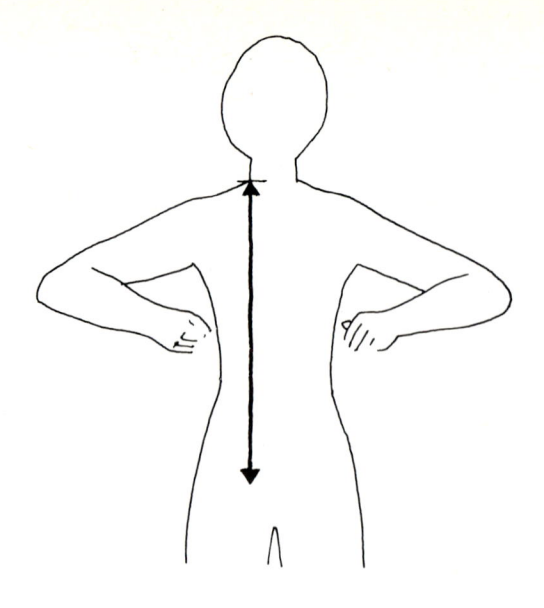

Figure 70.

LENGTH OF BODY ⎯⎯⎯⎯⎯⎯⎯⎯⎯⎯⎯⎯⎯→ LENGTH

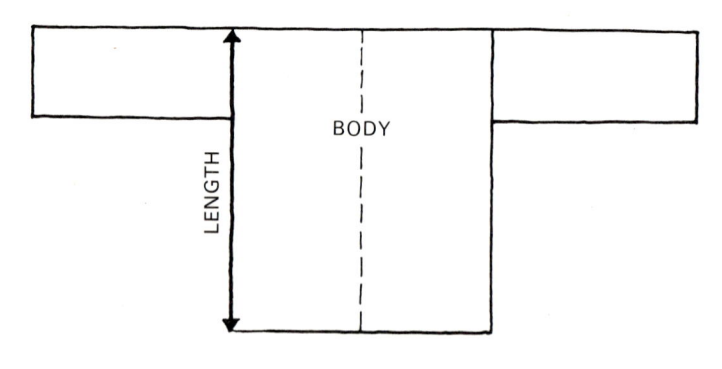

BODY

LENGTH

Figure 71.

The expression 'wing span' is used by Margrethe Hald in *Ancient Danish Textiles* of the distance from wrist to wrist. The wing span is measured round the back of the neck from wrist to wrist, with the arms lifted and bent slightly forward.

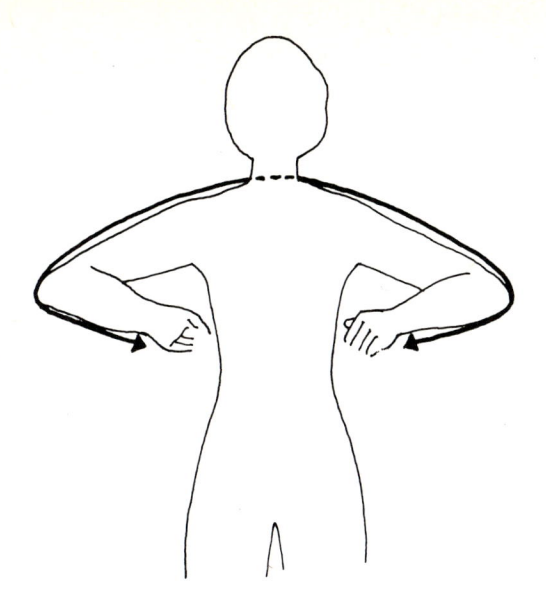

Figure 72.

WING SPAN (WS) MINUS BREADTH OF BODY ⟶ 2 SLEEVE LENGTHS

$$\frac{\text{WS MINUS BREADTH OF BODY}}{2} \longrightarrow \text{SLEEVE LENGTH}$$

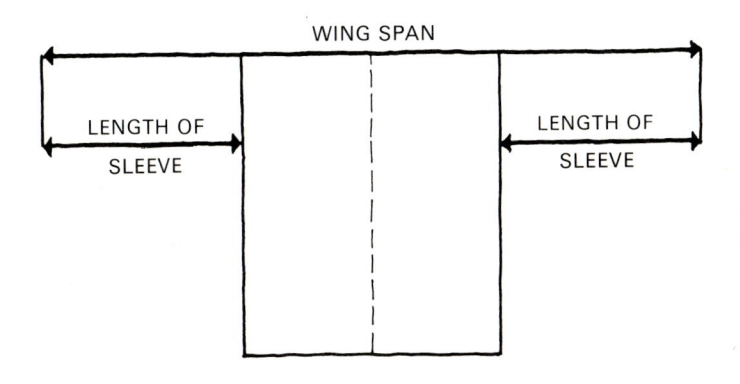

Figure 73.

It is not necessary to calculate the length of the sleeves in all cases. If the body and sleeves are cut out of one piece of material, the wing span is marked out symmetrically in relation to the centre of the body.

NECKHOLE

The neckhole can be a horizontal or vertical cut or a hole of any shape. In all cases the neckhole must be wide enough to allow the head to pass through and a tight-fitting neckhole should always be provided with a slit.

In order for a round, tight-fitting neckhole to be placed correctly in relation to the position of the neck on the body it has to be shifted forward a little in relation to the shoulder line. When sketching in the round neckhole on the body it is necessary to know the diameter of the planned neckhole. This is calculated on the basis of the width round the neck.

The circumference of a circle is $2\pi r$, where r is the radius and 2r the diameter. This formula can be simplified and with sufficient accuracy it can be said that

$$\frac{\text{WIDTH ROUND THE NECK}}{3} \longrightarrow \text{DIAMETER OF THE NECKHOLE}$$

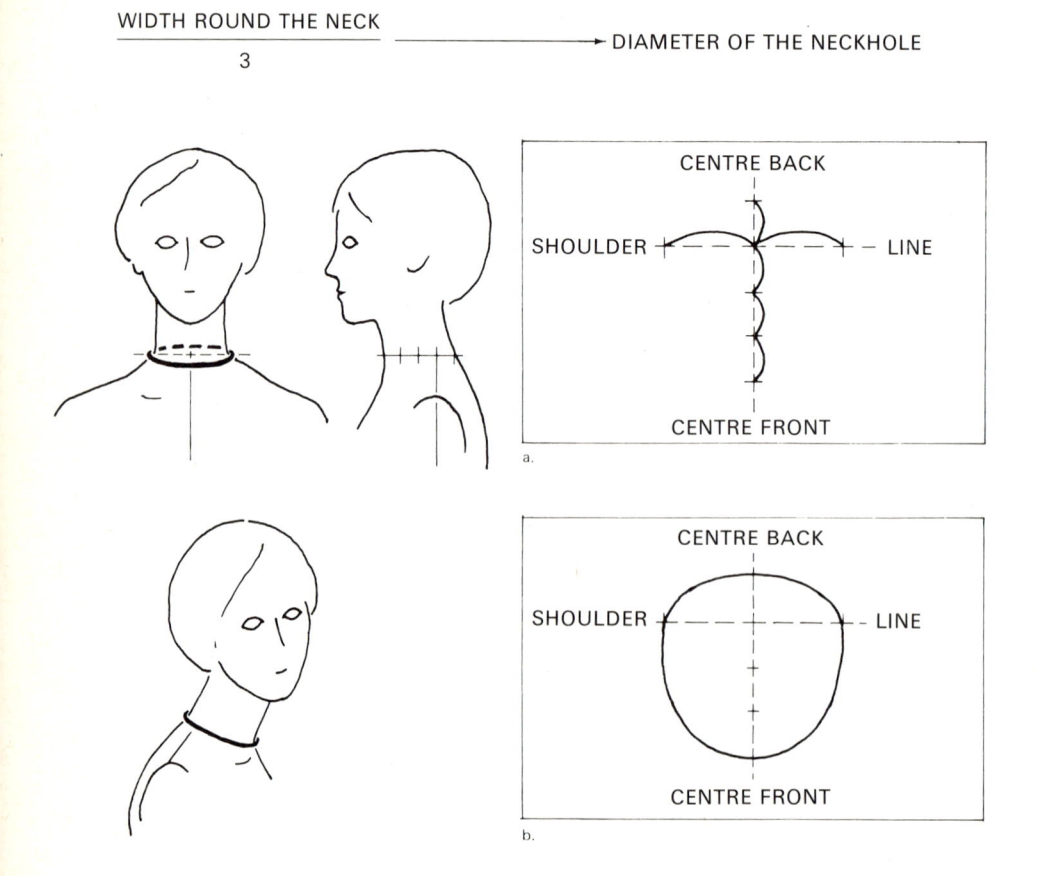

Figure 74.

The position of the neckhole on the body is shown in figs. a and b, above. Here the neckhole has been shifted forward in relation to the shoulder line so that a quarter of the diameter is behind the shoulder line and three quarters is in front of it.

The position of the neckhole depends on the wearer's posture. The further forward the neck is carried in relation to the rest of the body, the further forward the neckhole has to be shifted so that, for example, a fifth of the diameter may be behind the shoulder line and four fifths may be in front of it.

HOOD

The simplest hood has a quadrangular shape. It is drawn on the basis of the biggest height and width measurements of the head. The hood can be used in connection with a horizontal as well as a round neckhole as long as the width of the neckhole is adapted to the width of the hood. The hood fits a horizontally cut neckhole better if the hole is slightly rounded in front.

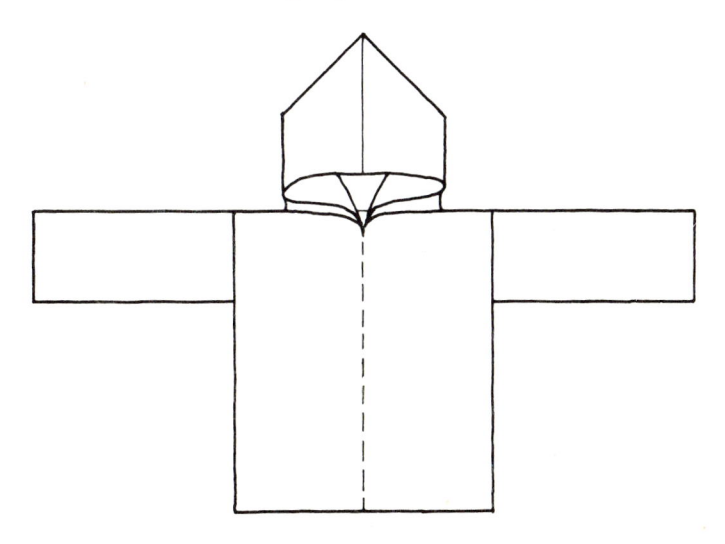

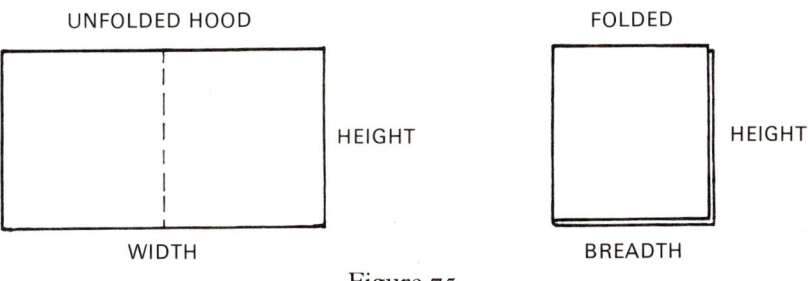

Figure 75.

WIDTH OF HEAD ⟶ WIDTH OF HOOD

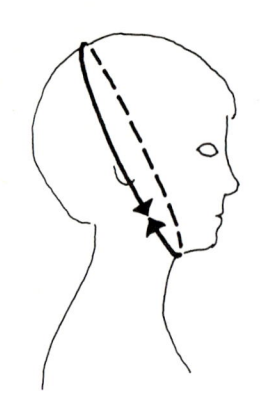

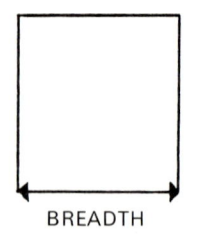

$\dfrac{\text{WIDTH}}{2}$ ⟶ BREADTH

BREADTH

DOUBLE HEIGHT OF HEAD / 2 ⟶ HEIGHT OF HOOD

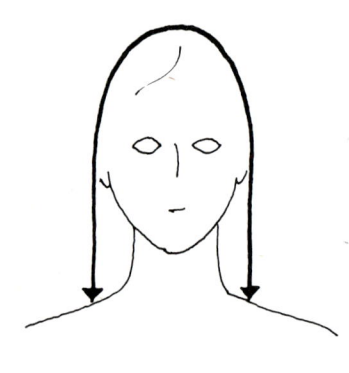

HEIGHT

Figure 76.

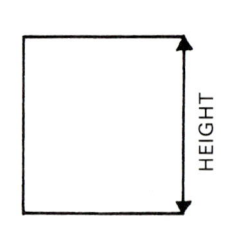

SUGGESTIONS FOR CALCULATION OF EXTRA WIDTH

WB = Width of body
WA = Width of arm
I Tight-fitting basic shape
II Loose basic shape
III Wide basic shape

	Extra width		
	I	II	III
Width of body +	1/12 WB	1/6 WB	1/4 WB
Width of arm +	1/6 WA	1/3 WA	1/2 WA

(See fig. 78 for the calculation of the basic measures to be used when drawing the three basic shapes).

	Extra width		
	I	II	III
WB 96 cm +	8 cm	16 cm	24 cm
WA 30 cm +	5 cm	10 cm	15 cm

Figure 77.

See below for the chart of body measurements and the calculations to be used when drawing up the three basic shapes. For the calculation of extra widths see fig. 77 and the diagrams for personal use on p. 112.

Body measurements	Calculations	Basic measurements
Width of body	$\dfrac{WB + \text{extra width}}{2}$	Width of body
Width of arm	$\dfrac{WA + \text{extra width}}{2}$	Width of sleeve
Length		Length of body
Wing span	$\dfrac{WS - \text{width of body}}{2}$	Length of sleeve
Width round the neck	$\dfrac{\text{Width round the neck}}{3}$	Diameter of neckhole
Width round the head	$\dfrac{\text{Width round the head}}{2}$	Breadth of hood
Double height of head	$\dfrac{\text{Double height of head}}{2}$	Height of hood

WB = Width of body   WA = Width of arm   WS = Wing span

An example: THE TIGHT-FITTING BASIC SHAPE I

Body measurements		Calculations	Basic measurements	
Width of body	96 cm	$\dfrac{96 + 8}{2}$	52 cm	Width of body
Width of arm	30 cm	$\dfrac{30 + 5}{2}$	17½ cm	Width of sleeve
Length	60 cm		60 cm	Length of body
Wing span	170 cm	$\dfrac{140 - 52}{2}$	44 cm	Length of sleeve
Width round the neck	36 cm	$\dfrac{36}{3}$	12 cm	Diameter of neckhole
Width round the head	66 cm	$\dfrac{66}{2}$	33 cm	Breadth of hood
Double height of head	70 cm	$\dfrac{70}{2}$	35 cm	Height of hood

Figure 78.

PROCEDURE FOR DRAWING THE THREE BASIC SHAPES AND THE QUADRANGULAR HOOD

1. Take body measurements (page 74). Read 'The function of the basic shape' (page 72).
2. Fill in the three diagrams on page 112.
3. Draw all three basic shapes on thick paper (see below).
4. Draw, and possibly cut, a cardboard template of the neckhole, clearly marking shoulder and centre lines (page 78).
5. Draw a quadrangular hood on thick paper (fig. 76).
6. Choose one of the three basic shapes as a basis for the garment desired (page 72). Note that it will often be necessary to increase the length of the sleeve when the wide basic shape is used for top garments.
7. Draw the variation according to the above points (page 83).

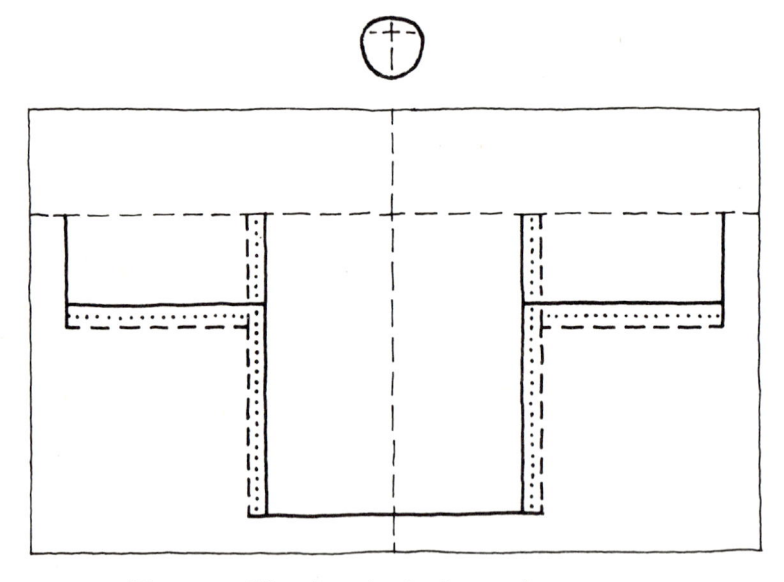

Figure 79. The three basic shapes drawn out on brown paper. Make the neckhole template in cardboard.

Variations on the basic shape

GENERAL FEATURES OF FORM

It can be difficult to view the many drawings of types of garments as a whole. What follows therefore is a discussion of the individual features of the form of the garments, in which these features are examined independently of the stylistically distinctive mark of individual countries.

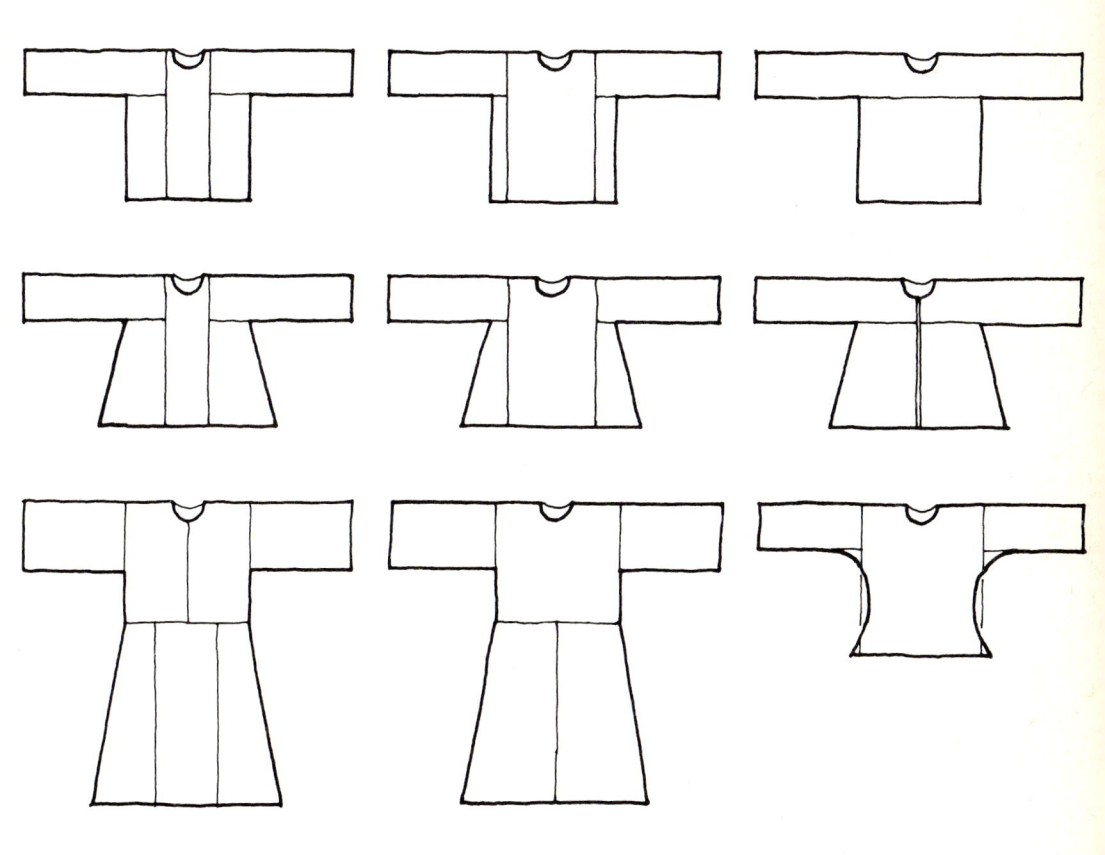

Figure 80.

Notice how the width of the material can influence the shape and lines of the garments. (See also page 68).
What practical considerations are there if the garment is made from small pieces of material?
What aesthetic considerations are there if the garment is intended to hide or to emphasise, for example?

LENGTH, WIDTH, CUTS WITHIN THE OUTLINES OF THE SHAPES

Figure 81.

The examples illustrate that the length of the garments can be varied according to need.
What requirements will make a difference to the width?
Is it important that the bottom edge is rounded off in some cases? (See also fig. 92).
One of the examples has gathers.

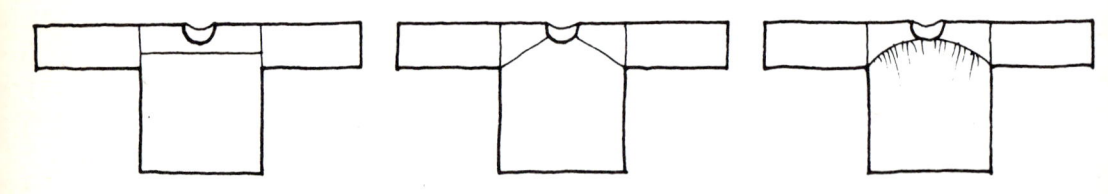

Figure 82.

What advantages are there in an article of clothing which has gathers? (See also page 92).
Is it evident that the body part can be divided in two across the top in some cases. The top piece is called a yoke if it is stitched to the lower part of the body. When the top piece is an extra layer sewn onto the body at the shoulder line it is called a shoulder piece.

SLEEVES

What does the shape of the sleeve tell us about the function of a garment? (Compare the examples given in the first row with those in the second).

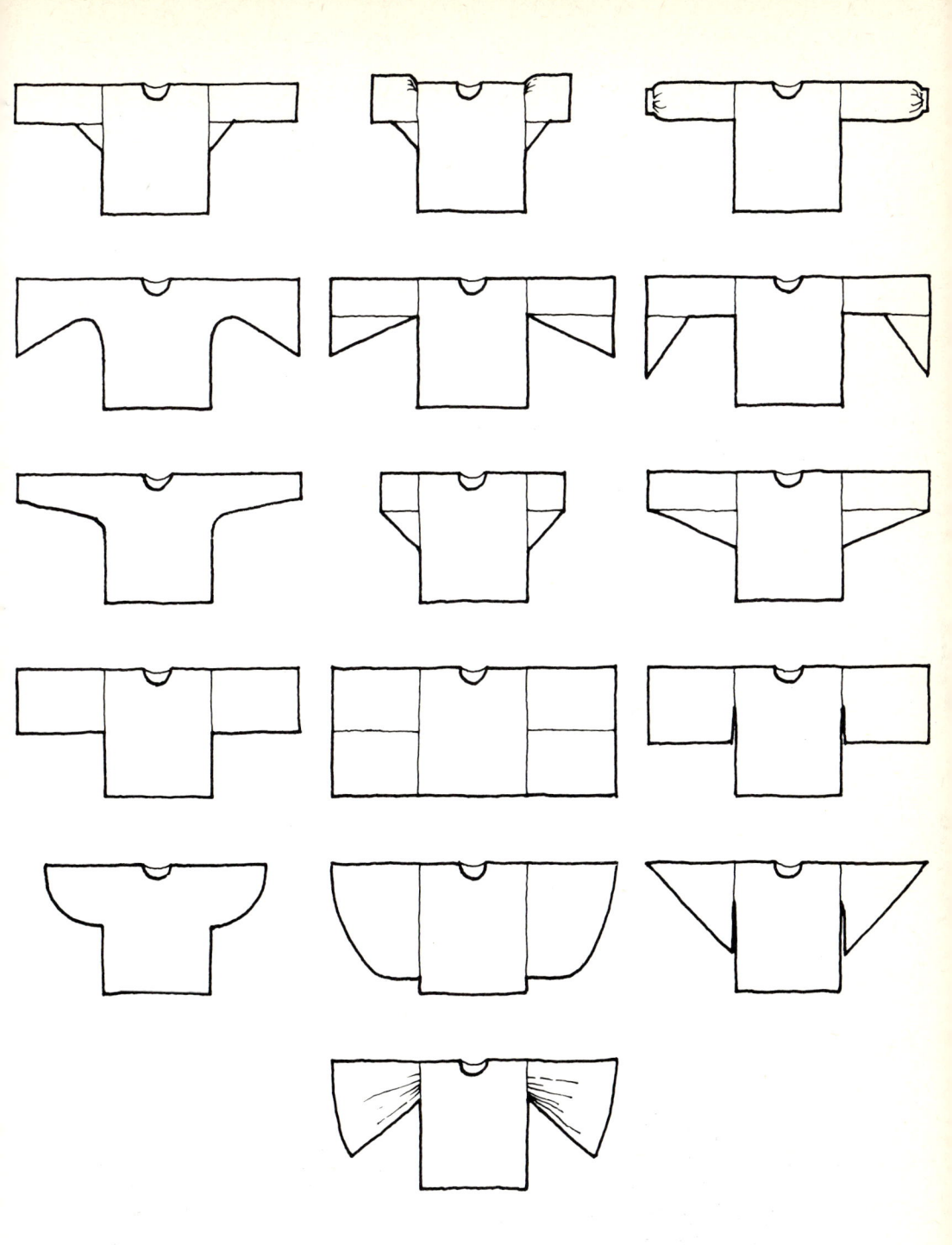

Figure 83.

ARMHOLES

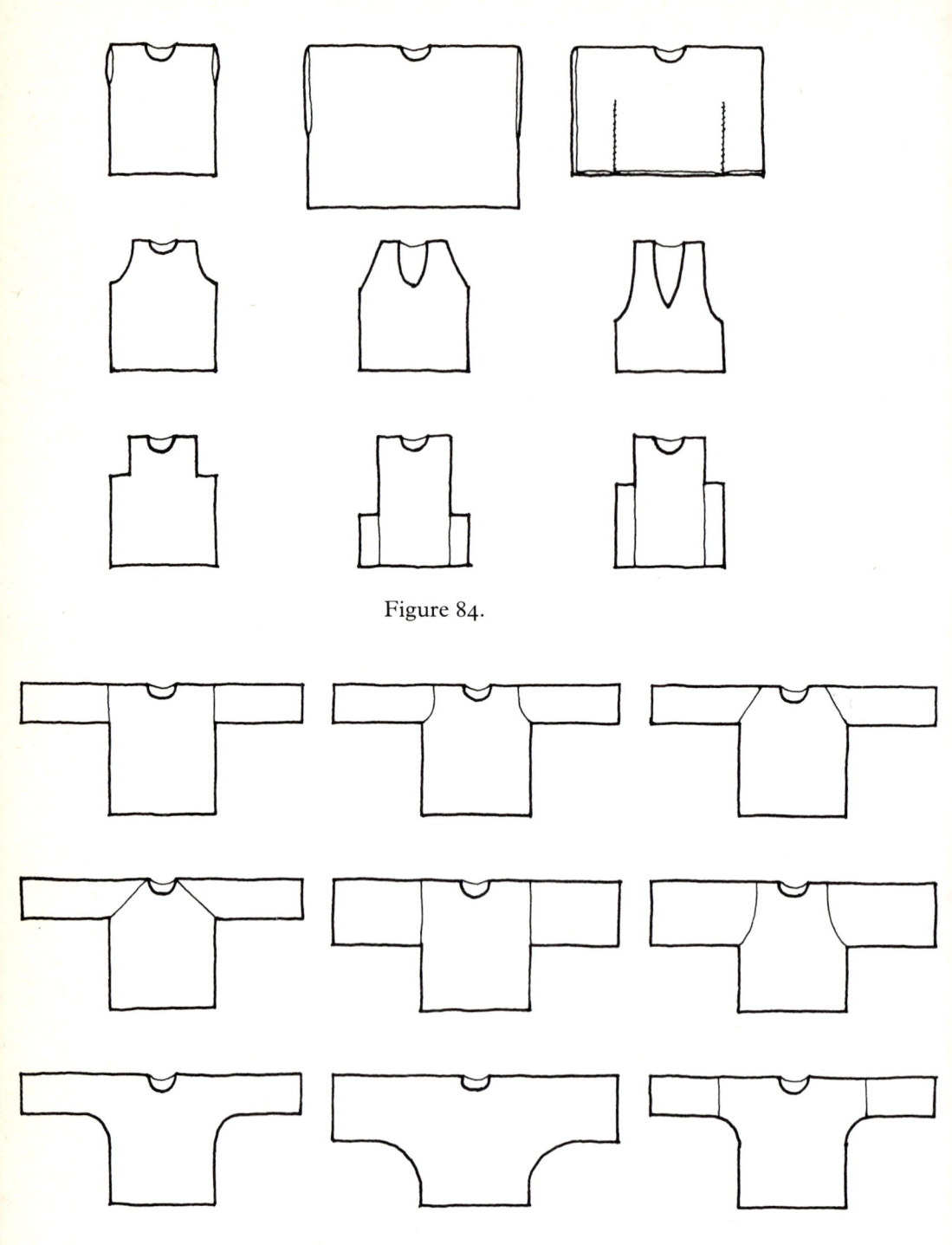

Figure 84.

Figure 85.

What assumptions about climatic conditions can be made on the basis of the examples given left?
Note that the example in the second and third rows can be worn on top of something else.

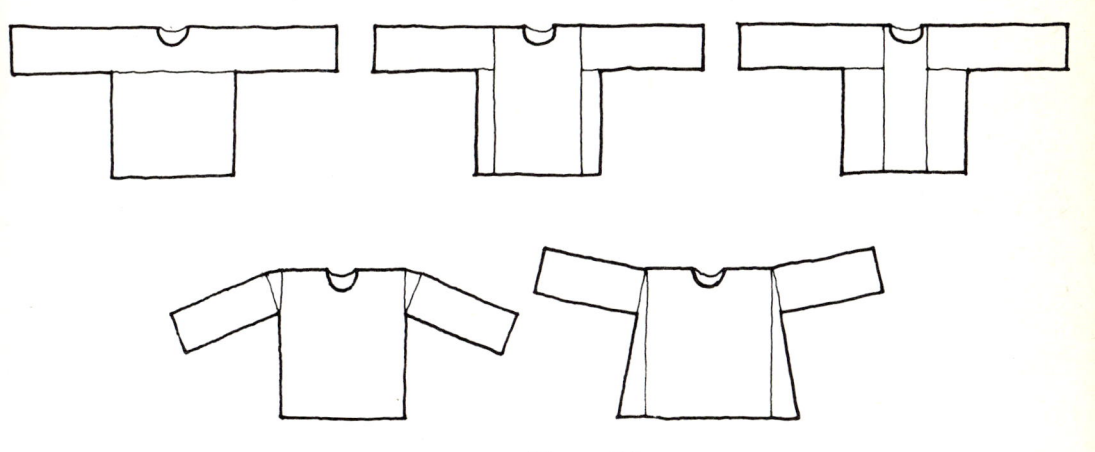

Figure 86.

Note how the width of the material can influence the way in which the sleeves are attached to the body. (See especially the top row on this page).
Which function do the gussets have in the last two examples? (See also page 65).
The gussets under the sleeves of the garment are square in some cases, rhomboid in others.

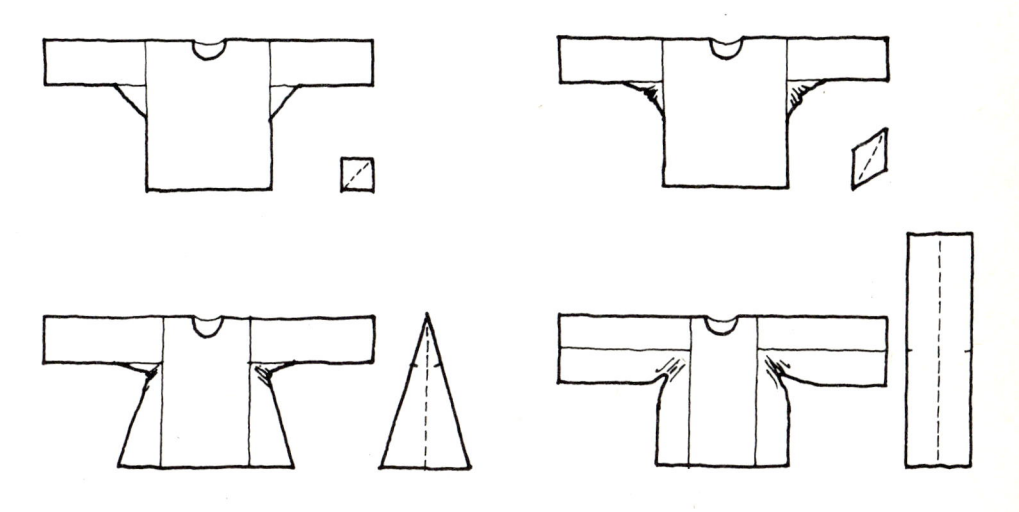

Figure 87.

How does the shape of the gussets influence the function of the garment? (See also page 91).

In the last example the garment is given greater width under the arms by making the sidepieces continue into the sleeves. What does this imply as regards choice of material?

FRONT OPENINGS

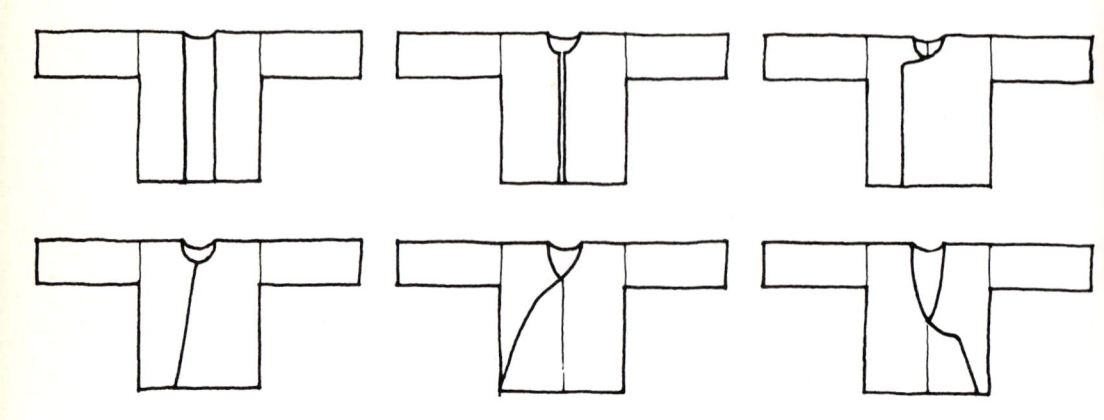

Figure 88.

The piece of material which reaches across the actual centre line at the centre opening in front is called a flap. In caftan types there is, as a rule, only a flap in the top front half. Note the various shapes of the flap and the ways of stitching it on.

Is it possible to cut the flap and the front half out of one piece of material?

NECKHOLES

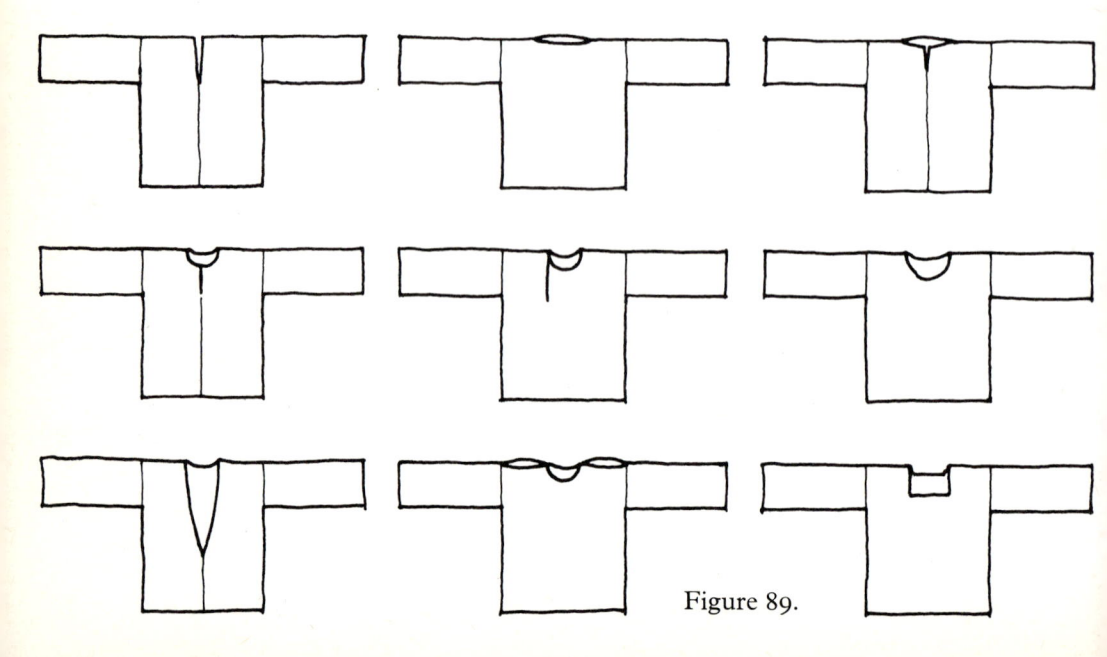

Figure 89.

Of what importance is the position of the neckhole in relation to the shoulder line?
Find examples of different kinds of slits.

COLLARS AND HOODS

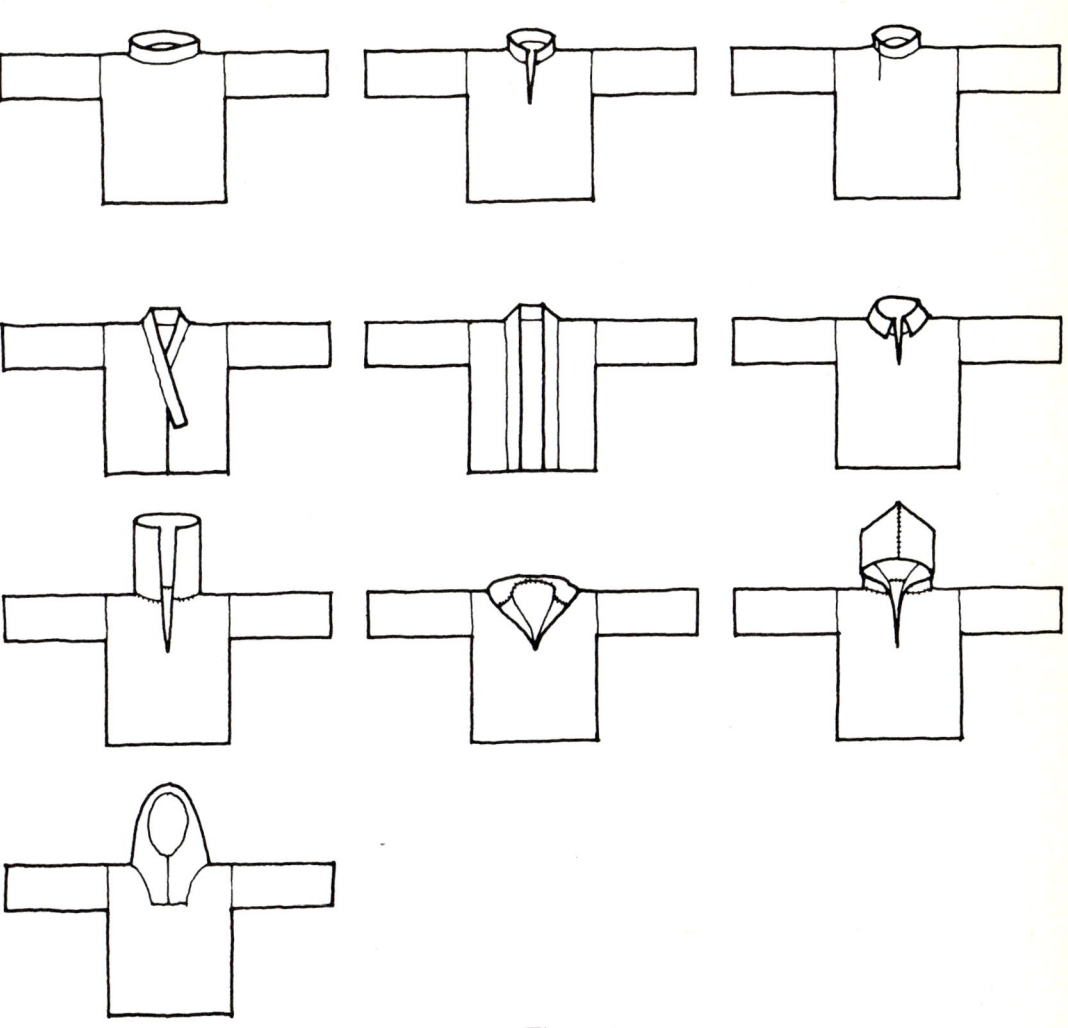

Figure 90.

What are the functions of the two different types of hoods?
   The hood of the anorak is perhaps the example which is most difficult to work out. See page 93 for further guidance.

Drawing the variations

A number of the details and variations discussed in the section on general features of form are easy to incorporate. What follows therefore, is a description of a few very common variations of the basic shape.

ARMHOLES

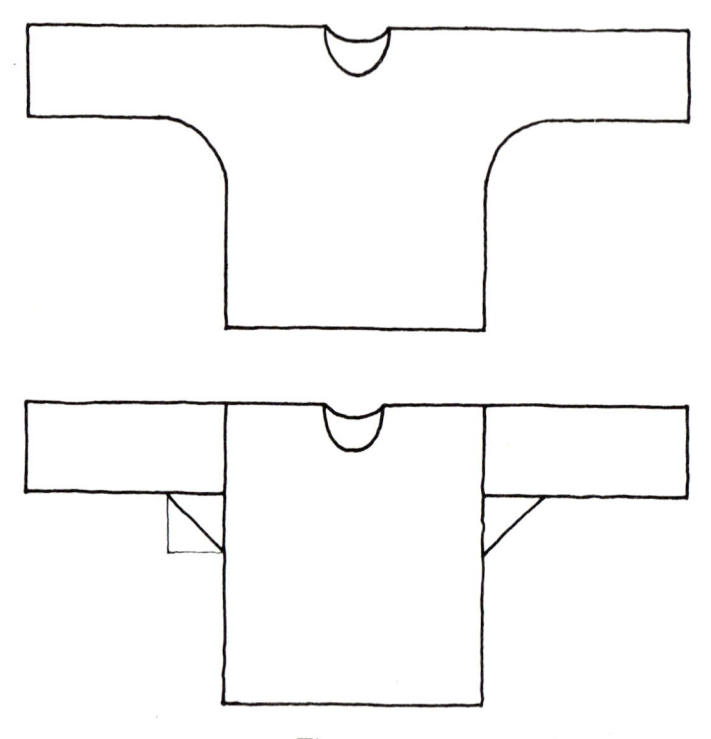

Figure 91.

If greater freedom of movement is needed in the basic shape, the garment can be rounded under the arms or gussets can be inserted.

The simplest and most commonly used sleeve gusset is a square which is folded diagonally. The size of the square is of course dependent on the type of garment and on the choice of material. Experience shows, though, that if the side measure of the square gusset corresponds to a fifth or a quarter of the breadth of the body it will fit most people. This measure can also be used to delimit the curve under the arm.

LENGTH AND WIDTH, CUTS WITHIN THE OUTLINES OF THE SHAPES

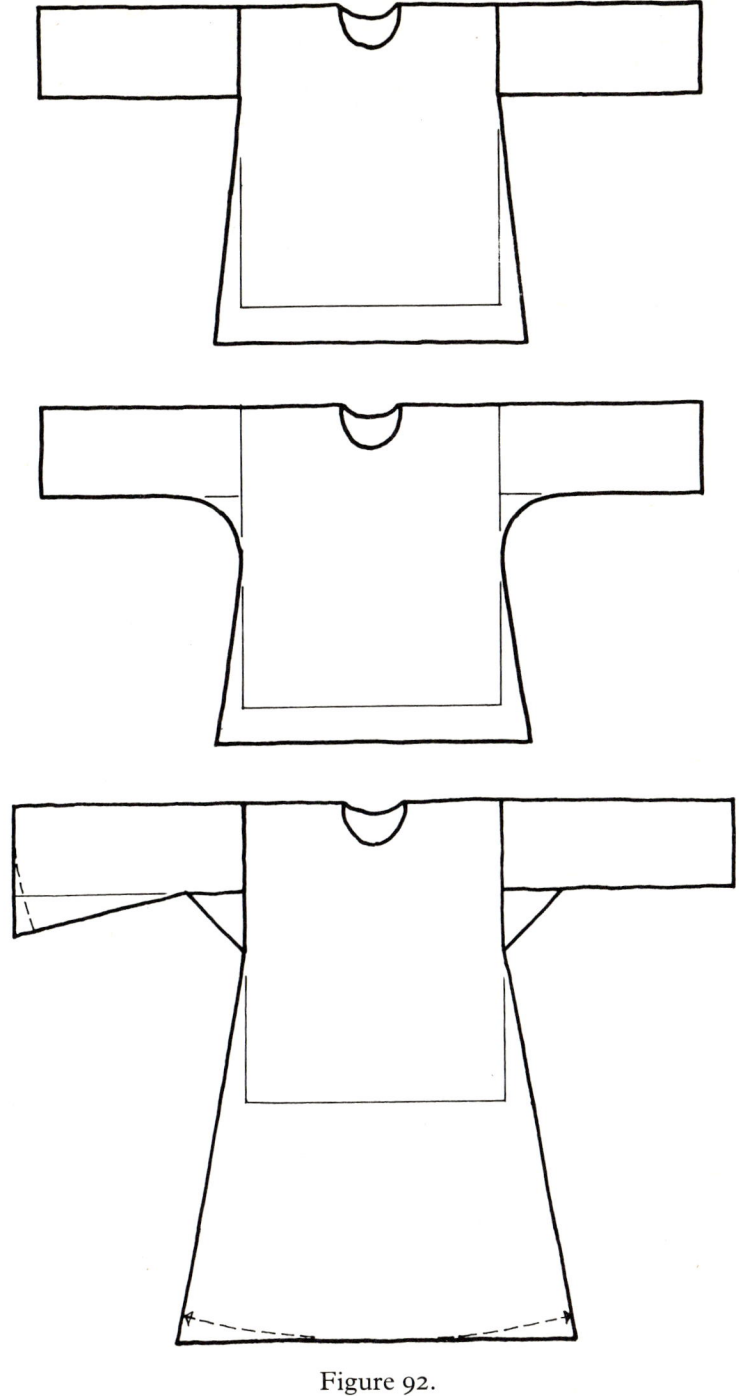

Figure 92.

The length of the body can be checked by measuring the distance from the floor to the bottom edge of the garment all the way round. The wearer stands upright in a natural position while somebody else checks the length.

The bottom edge of a very wide garment must be rounded off if an even length all the way round is required. The same is true of a very wide sleeve.

If the garment is intended to cover the hips, check whether the body width is large enough. In many cases it may be necessary to cut the sides on the bias or to make slits.

The garment will not hang well if the sides are cut too much on the bias. If the garment is to be very wide it is necessary, therefore, to cut the front and the back in the centre and place some of the width here.

If the sleeves of the garment, or, for example, the lower part of the body, are to have pleats or gathers, this width is added in the middle of the relevant section of the garment.

By cutting through and stitching the sleeves or the body together again, lengthwise or crosswise, simple decorative variations can be obtained without changing the fit.

If, at the same time, width is added at the cut (in the form of gathers or pleats) in conjunction with a yoke, for example, it is possible to position the width exactly where it is needed.

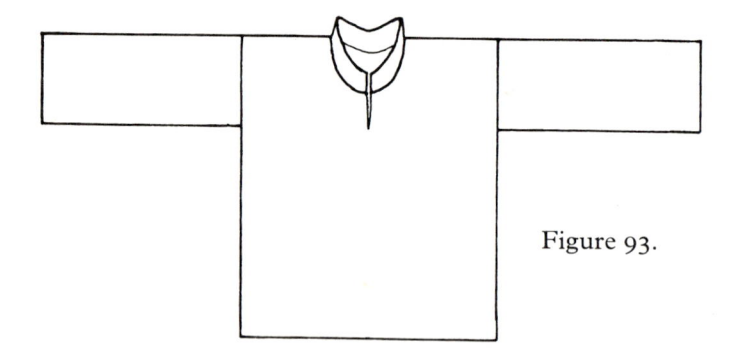

Figure 93.

COLLARS AND HOODS

The simplest collar is quadrangular. Its width must correspond to that of the neckhole, which can be measured with a tape held edgeways.

The collar can have many different heights. If it becomes too high to stand on its own it can be folded down.

The quadrangular collar can be fitted into all kinds of neckholes provided that the width of the collar is adapted to the width of the neckhole. However, the collar will fit a horizontally cut neckhole better if the latter is slightly rounded in front.

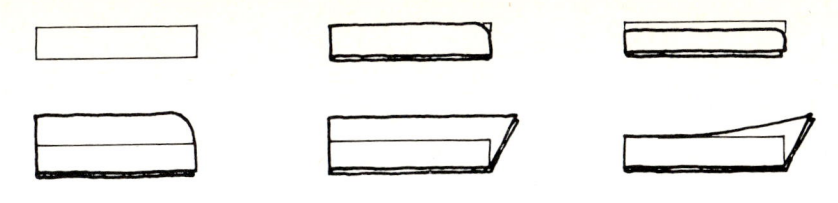

Figure 94.

As mentioned earlier the neckhole is adapted to the width of the hood. However, the hood can also to some extent be adapted to the neckhole by making a couple of pleats at the back and sides of it when stitching it to the body.

In Gudmund Hatt's *Arctic Skin-clothes* the lowest part of the anorak hood is referred to as its root. It is up to you how long and how broad the root is to be (page 102).

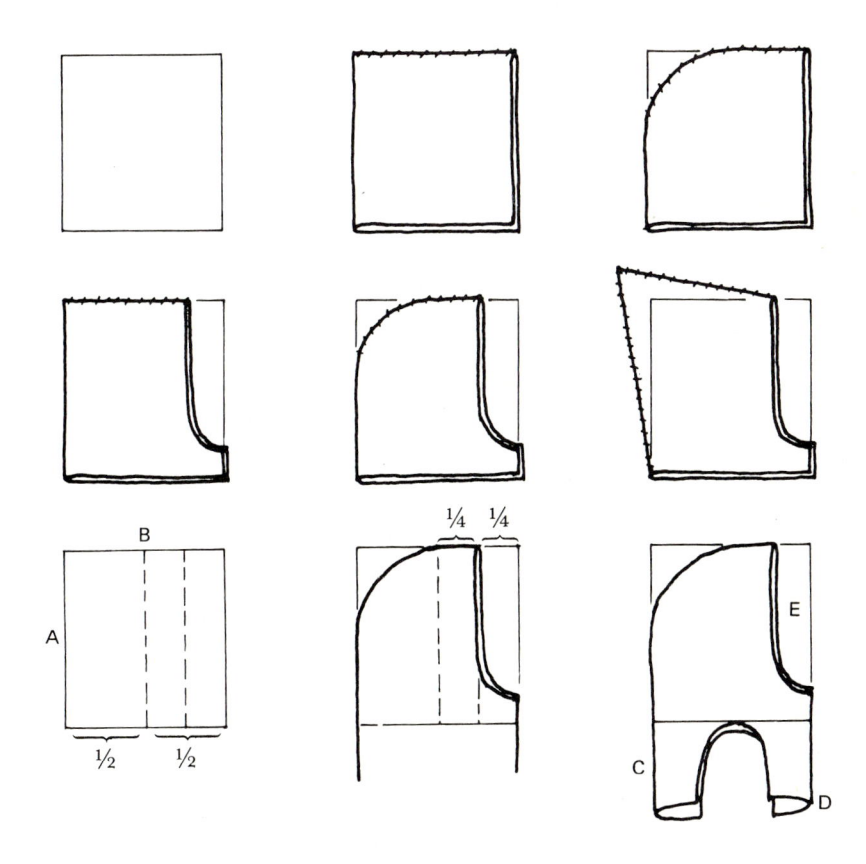

Figure 95. A = height of hood. B = breadth of hood. C = length of root of the hood. D = breadth of root of the hood. E = width of the head.

93

PROCEDURE FOR DRAWING VARIATIONS OF GARMENTS

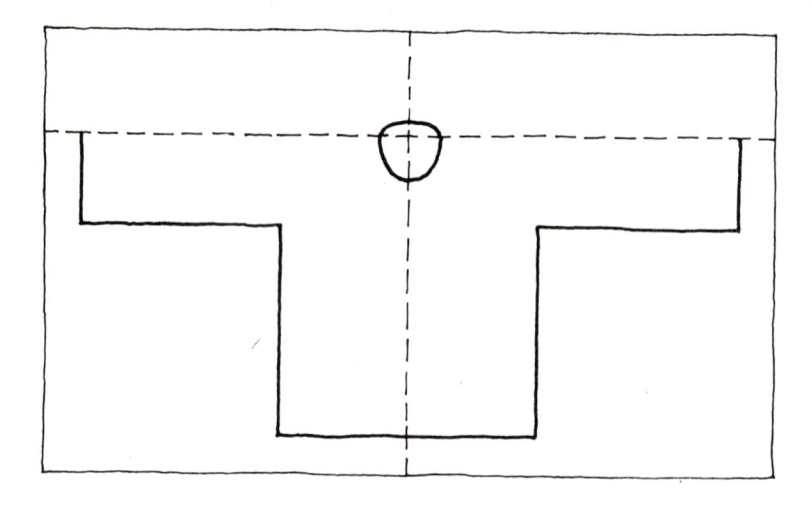

Figure 96. Tissue paper copy of the basic shape with sketched-in neckhole.

1. Choose a basic shape (see page 72) and draw a copy on tissue paper so that the shoulder line is placed far enough from the top edge of the paper to allow room for drawing the neckhole as shown above and perhaps a complete unfolded sleeve as shown on page 95.
2. Draw the neckhole on the body according to the neck template (page 82).
3. If necessary, draw a copy of the quadrangular hood on tissue paper (page 82).
4. Sketch in the desired variations on the tissue paper. As a rule the same amendments are drawn on both the front and back of the body. At times, however, the front and the back have to be so different that it might be an advantage to draw two copies of the body.
   In order to be able to draw a flap it is necessary, for example, to cut the centre line of the body.
   It is a good idea to draw a complete sleeve on the tissue-paper copy if there are variations on where the sleeves are to be stitched to the body (see fig. 97). This facilitates the subsequent working process when the various parts of the pattern are put on the material and cut out.
   For the same reason a pattern is also drawn for a complete yoke and a complete collar.

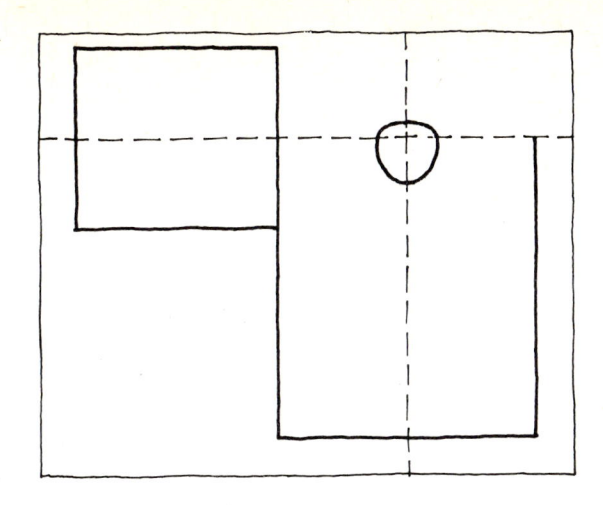

Figure 97. Tissue paper copy of the body of the basic shape with sketched-in neckhole and complete sleeve.

Suggestion for order of priorities in drawing variations:
Sleeve gusset or curve
Length of sleeve
Width of sleeve
Place at which sleeve is attached to the body
Length of body
Width of body
New cuts within the outlines of the pattern
Hood
Neckhole
Front opening
Flap
Collar

If one of the types of clothing discussed in this book is to form the basis for variations, the basic shape on page 15 can, with advantage, be compared with the relevant schematic drawing since they have been drawn to the same scale (1/15).

It might seem superfluous to start by drawing on tissue paper in the case of something as simple as a rectangular kanga, or peplus, or a poncho. but if you want to get an idea of the dimensions of the garment in relation to the body and the position of a possible decoration, the paper is a help.

Examples

KANGA VARIATION

1. Measure the length from waist to foot.
2. Draw a rectangle on tissue paper, one side being the measured length and the other 1½ times the width of the body.

PEPLUS VARIATION

1. Measure the wing span from elbow to elbow (page 77).
2. Measure the length from shoulder to foot.
3. Draw a rectangle on tissue paper, one side being the measured length and the other twice the measured wing span.
4. Gather the rectangle to form a cylinder.

PONCHO VARIATION

1. Measure the length from shoulder to knee.
2. Measure the wing span from elbow to elbow (page 77).
3. Draw a rectangle on tissue paper, one side being twice the measured length, the other being the measured wing span.
4. Draw a slit for the neckhole in the middle of the rectangle. Use the neck template (page 78).

BRONZE AGE BLOUSE VARIATION

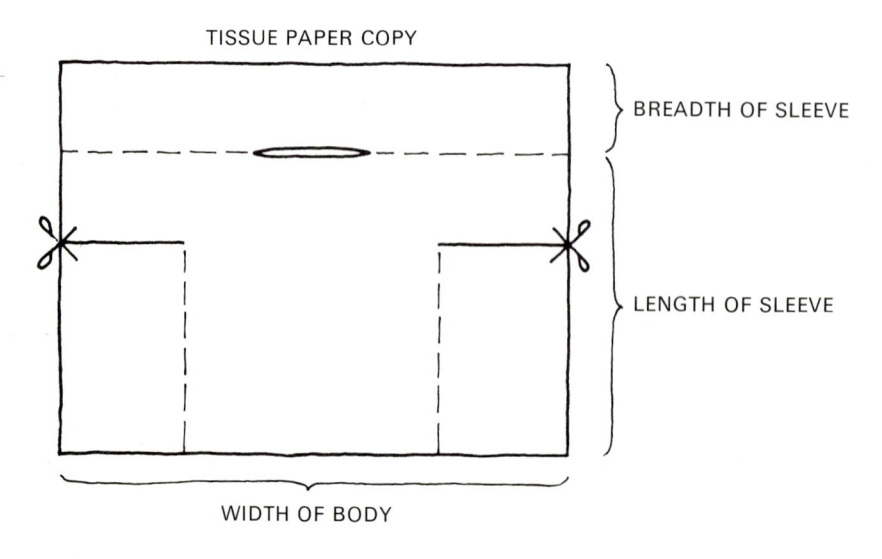

TISSUE PAPER COPY

BREADTH OF SLEEVE

LENGTH OF SLEEVE

WIDTH OF BODY

                    FRONT   BACK

Figure 98.

1. Choose a basic shape (page 73).
2. Draw a rectangle on tissue paper, one side being the width of the body, the other the length of the body plus the breadth of the sleeve.
3. Draw folding lines as shown on the drawing.
4. Draw cutting lines as shown on the drawing.
5. Draw neckhole as on the drawing or possibly according to the neck template (page 78).
6. Cut, fold and try on the basic shape.

Pin up and sew

JELLABA VARIATION

1. Choose a basic shape and draw two copies of the body and one copy of a complete sleeve on tissue paper (page 95).
2. Draw a sleeve gusset (page 90).
3. Lengthen the body (page 91).
4. Slant cut the sides of the body (page 91).
5. Draw a copy of the quadrangular hood (page 80).
6. Draw a horizontal neckhole which corresponds to the width of the hood. The neckhole is rounded a little in front. See also page 79.
7. Cut the body front at the centre.
8. Draw and cut a straight strip for the flap. Tape the flap to one of the front halves.
9. Draw pockets.

Pin and sew.

FRONT

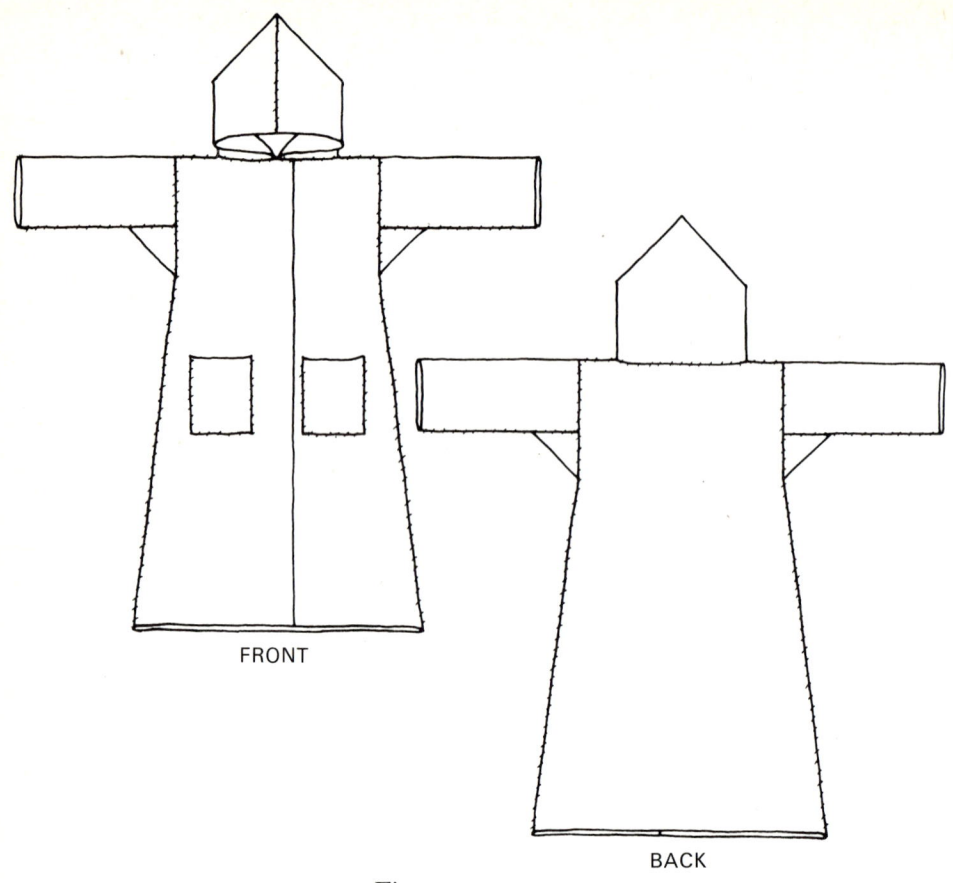

BACK

Figure 99.

TUNIC VARIATION (BLOUSE)

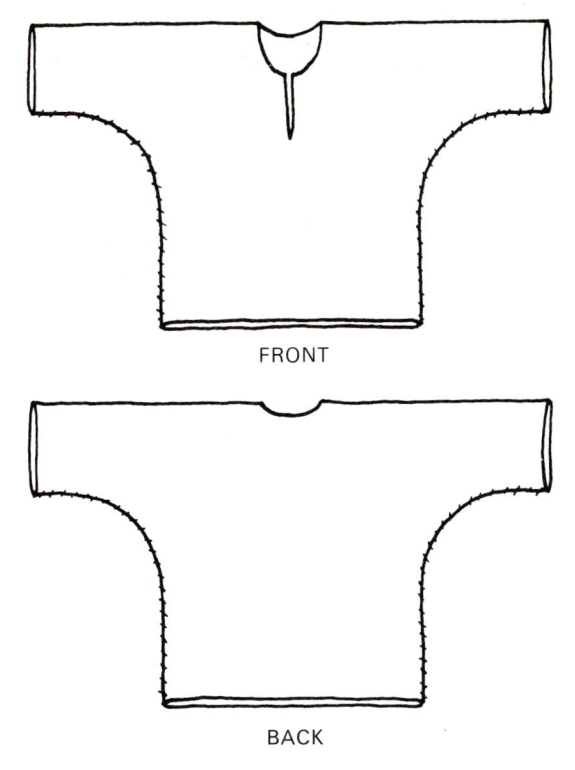

FRONT

BACK

Figure 100.

1. Choose a basic shape and draw a copy on tissue paper (page 96).
2. Draw curves under the arms (page 91).
3. Remove the lines at which the sleeves would normally be attached to the body.
4. Mark the length of the sleeves, which is determined by the width of the material.
5. Draw a neckhole with a slit at the centre in front. Use the neck template (page 78).

Cut out and sew.

TUNIC VARIATION (SHIRT)

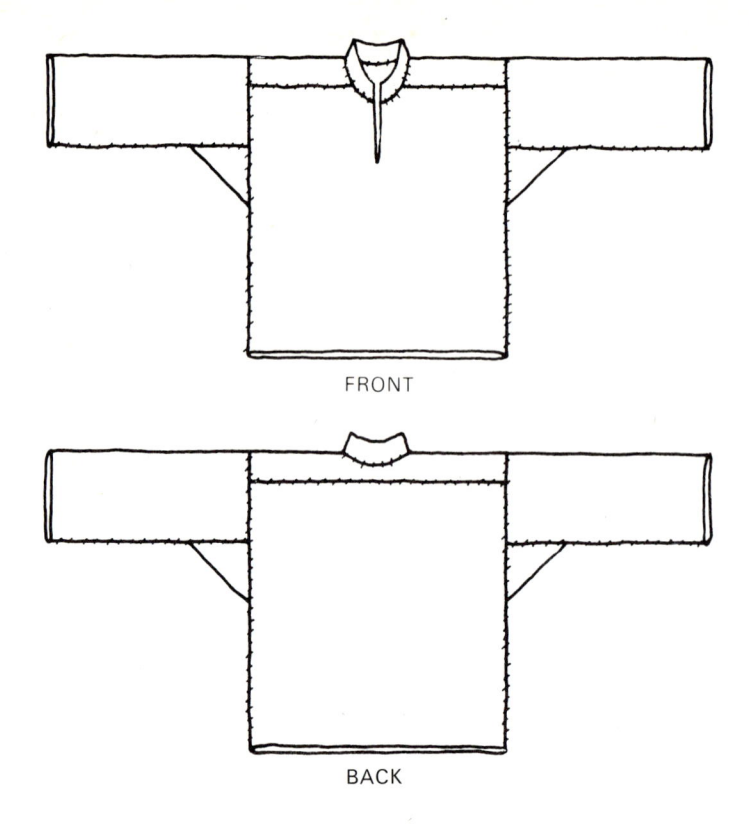

FRONT

BACK

Figure 101.

1. Choose a basic shape and draw a copy of the body and a complete sleeve on tissue paper (page 95).
2. Draw a sleeve gusset (page 90).
3. Draw a complete shoulder piece (page 84 and page 96).
4. Draw a neckhole with a slit at the centre in front. Use the neck template (page 78).
5. Draw a complete collar.

Cut out and sew.

TUNIC VARIATION (DRESS)

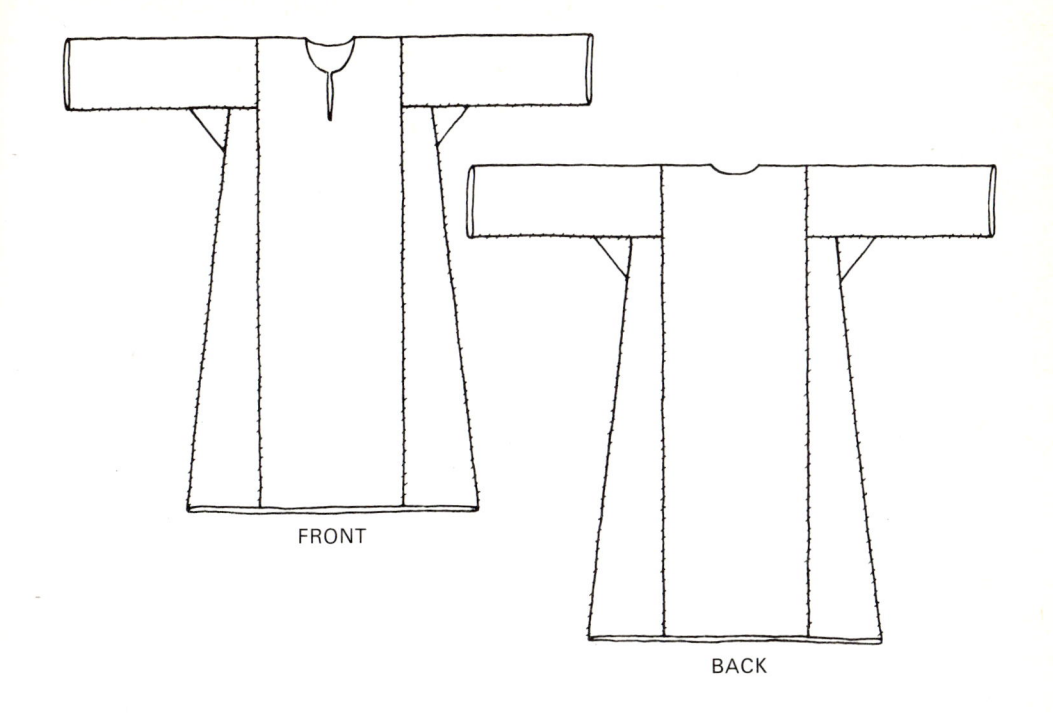

Figure 102.

1. Choose a basic shape and draw a copy of the body and a complete sleeve on tissue paper (page 95).
2. Draw a sleeve gusset (page 90).
3. Lengthen the body (page 91).
4. Slant cut the sides of the body.
5. Draw a new, narrower breadth for the body.
6. Lengthen the sleeves so that they reach the inner breadth of the body.
7. In this way the side gussets are defined and new lines at which the sleeves are to be attached are drawn.
8. Draw a neckhole with a slit at the centre in front. Use the neck template (page 78).
9. If necessary, round off the bottom edge of the body.

Cut out and sew.

ANORAK VARIATION

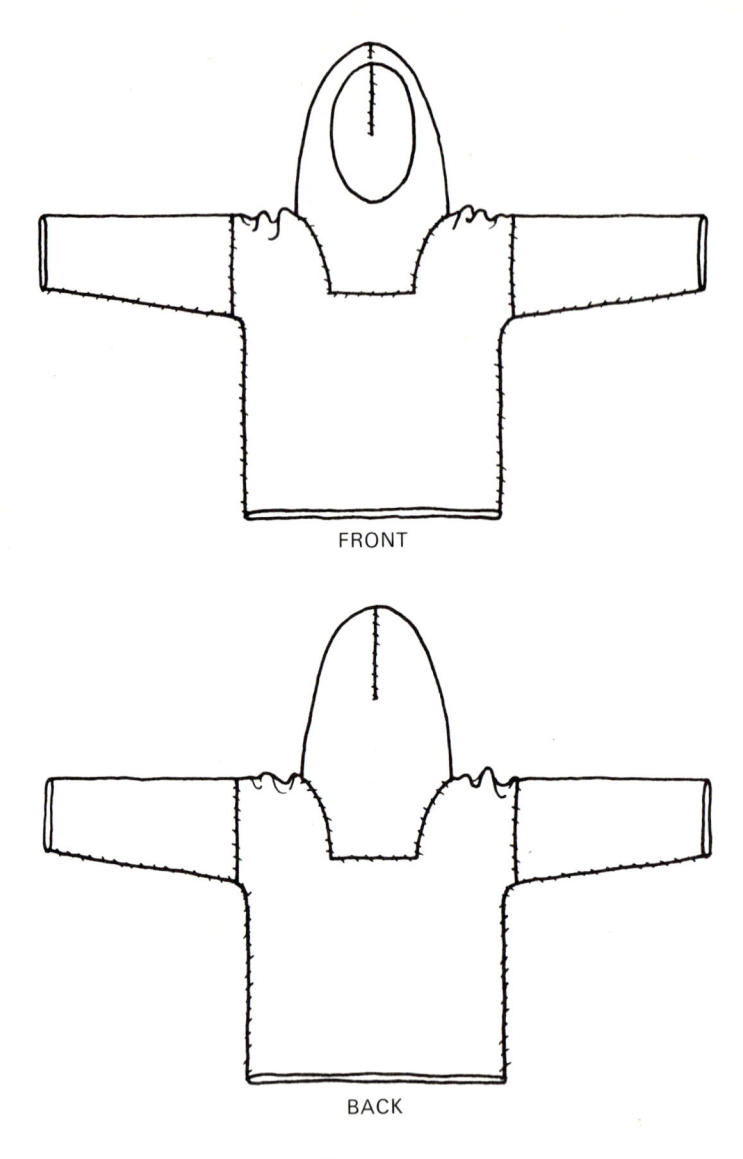

FRONT

BACK

Figure 103.

1. Choose a basic shape and draw a copy on tissue paper (page 95).
2. Draw curves under the arms (page 91).
3. Draw new lines at which the sleeves are to be attached. See drawing.
4. Draw the sleeves so that they are narrow at the wrists.

5. Draw a copy of this changed basic shape and tape together the two parts at the shoulder line. Then cut off the sleeves.
6. Draw a copy of the quadrangular hood on tissue paper (page 80).
7. Draw the folding lines on the hood as shown on page 93.
8. Draw the curve of the hood at the back in the centre (page 93).
9. Draw the opening of the hood big enough for the head (page 93).
10. Draw the roots of the hood as long and as broad as desired (page 93).
11. Draw the shoulder curve of the hood comparatively flat (page 48 and page 93).
12. If necessary, try on a paper hood that has been securely taped together.
13. Draw a rectangle at the centre of the body; this indicates the position of the hood. The short side of the rectangle, which is the same length as the breadth of the bottom horizontal edge of the hood, is drawn parallel with the shoulder line. The long side of the rectangle, which is the same length as the shoulder curve of the hood, is drawn parallel with the centre lines at the front and at the back (page 48).

    Notice that the hood is stitched to the body before the rectangular neckhole is cut.

Cut and sew.

CAFTAN VARIATION

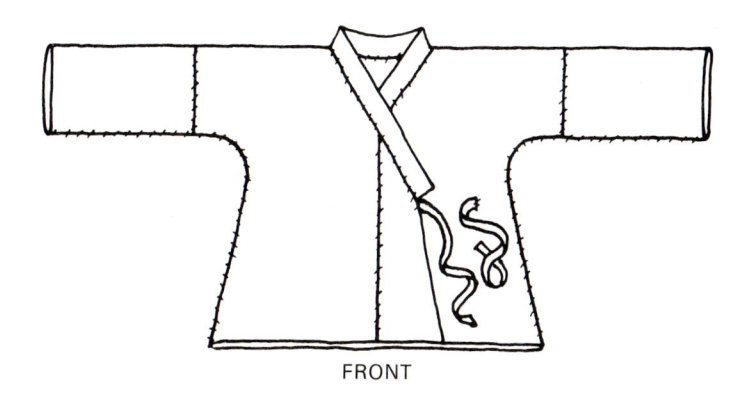

FRONT

Figure 104.

1. Choose a basic shape and draw a copy on tissue paper (page 94).
2. Draw curves under the arms (page 91).

BACK

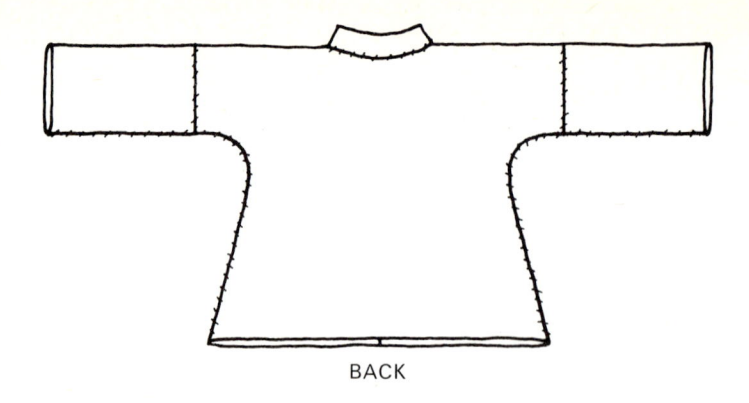

Figure 105.

3. Lengthen the body (page 91).
4. Slant cut the sides of the body (page 91).
5. Draw new lines at which the sleeves are to be stitched to the body.
6. Draw a copy of this changed basic shape and tape the two parts together at the shoulder line. Then cut off the sleeves from the body.
7. Draw neckhole. Use the neck template (page 78).
8. Cut the neckhole lower in front.
9. Cut the body front at the centre.
10. Draw and cut a flap and tape it to one of the front halves (page 88).
11. Try on the neckhole and flap and then separate the flap from the body again.
12. After the new neckhole has been measured with the tape held edgeways a complete collar is drawn (page 92 and page 93).

If one of the front halves of the body and the flap are cut out of one piece, i.e., without a seam at the centre in front, it will be necessary to stitch together the body at the shoulder lines or at the back in the centre.

Cut out and sew.

WAISTCOAT VARIATIONS

1. Choose a basic shape (see page 73) and draw a rectangle, one side being the length of the body, the other the double breadth of the body, i.e., the width of the body.
2. Sketch in the back-centre line (BC) and the side lines on the rectangle as shown on the drawing.

TISSUE PAPER COPY

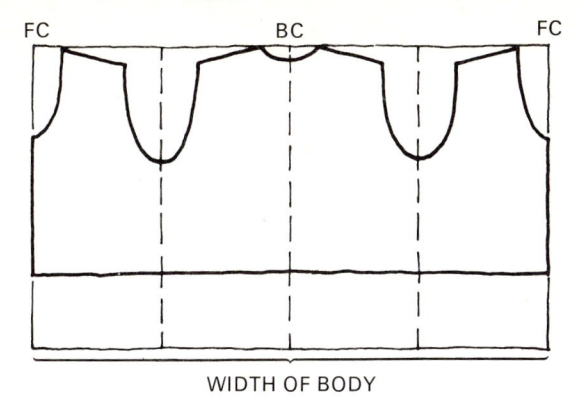

FC   BC   FC

WIDTH OF BODY

BC = BACK CENTRE
FC = FRONT CENTRE

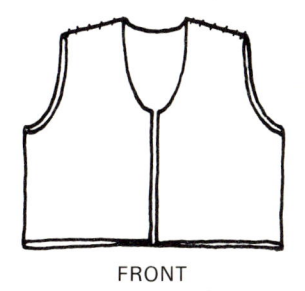

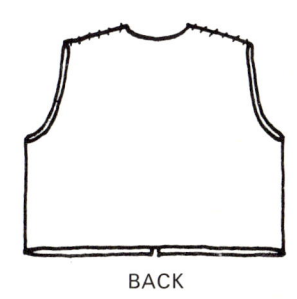

FRONT   BACK

Figure 106.

3. Draw the armholes as long as the breadth of the sleeve of the largest basic shape and enlarge them as desired (page 86).
4. Draw neckhole both on the front halves and on the back. Use the neck template (page 78).
5. Cut the neckhole lower in front.
6. Try on the armholes, the neckline and the length of the body.
7. If necessary, cut the shoulder lines so that they fit the body.
Cut out and sew.

Introduction to a method of working

The following deals with the use of fabric in making handbags—a subject closely connected with clothes.

AIMS

Imagine yourself in a museum, or with a number of pictures in front of you. The aim is to make a handbag which fulfils a certain function and which has been inspired by types of handbags from far and near.

Our aim is also to learn some basic facts about the concept of form, and become a little less dependent on ready-made patterns. Furthermore even a handbag is an expression of culture which can tell us something about other ways of life.

INVESTIGATIONS, INFORMATION AND ASSUMPTIONS

Start by sketching some handbags inspired by pictures or costume museum examples. The items must be carefully observed. Concentrate on varieties made of rectangles and, following this, try to find information about the background of the handbags.

Hunting and fishing nets can be seen as forerunners of the string bag. Far back in history the handbag and the string bag were tied to the clothes or to the naked body. In the last instance in particular, some kind of storage bag which could be hung on or tied to the body was needed.

The pocket, which makes very small handbags superfluous, is a comparatively late invention. It only appeared on the European fashion scene in the eighteenth century. Since then, the traditional combination has been: man—trousers, pocket; women—dress, handbag.

The distinctions between wrapping, net and container on the one hand, and handbag and pocket on the other are fluid.

HANDBAGS MADE OF QUADRANGULAR PIECES OF CLOTH

Each of these roughly sketched types of handbag has a tradition behind it, and following the introductory and scanty pieces of background information, it is natural to ask how the people, who needed precisely this or that particular type of handbag, lived. The answer may tell us something about the tools and materials available, and we could also get an idea of what was carried in the

Figure 107. A piece of cotton cloth from Japan, measuring 80 × 80 cm, and used to tie around objects as a primitive bag. *Photograph: Erik Jeppesen. The cloth is the property of Else Stephensen.*

NORTH AFRICA

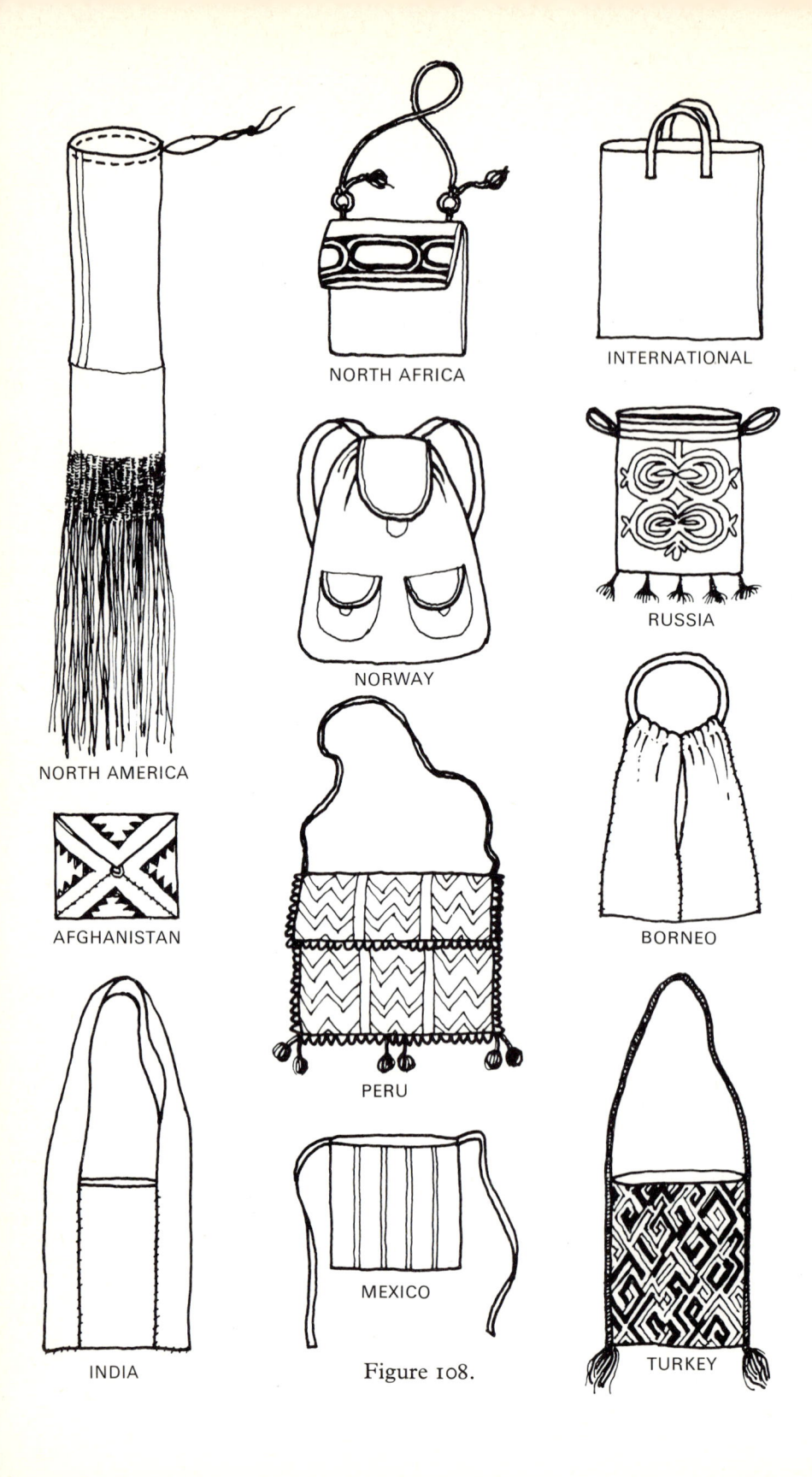

INTERNATIONAL

RUSSIA

NORWAY

NORTH AMERICA

AFGHANISTAN

PERU

BORNEO

INDIA

MEXICO

Figure 108.

TURKEY

bags. This again would yield information on proportions and on how it was probably carried.

We can now combine such assumptions and pieces of information with our own observation of the handbags.
The following questions might be asked:
Do the form and function of the individual handbag seem to be more important than the decoration?
Is a possible composition/decoration of a narrative, imaginative or ornamental nature?
How does it relate to the external form?
Is a possible connection between form and composition supported by the combination of colours?
What kind of material has been used?
How and with what kind of tools has it been made?
Where are the seams?
How many parts does the shape consist of?
What is the interrelation between the dimensions of the constituent parts like?

TESTING AND EVALUATION

We are still left with a number of unanswered questions. The more complex types of handbags cannot be understood without making them up. So, cut out in paper the individual constituent parts and then tape them together to see how they work. Repeated experiments will provide information on the structure of the handbag. At the same time they will confirm or invalidate our ideas about the function of the handbag.

SUMMING UP

Through extensive observation and experimentation we can perhaps draw up some general points on design and spatial shape in connection with handbags made of square or rectangular pieces.

Is it for example important for form and function that we calculate sufficient extra width in relation to capacity?
How long and how broad are the parts?
How many parts are used to make up the form?
How are the parts folded?
Where are the pieces left open and where are they stitched together?
Is the material soft or stiff?
Our knowledge of these things could be improved, but it is now broad enough for us to start work.

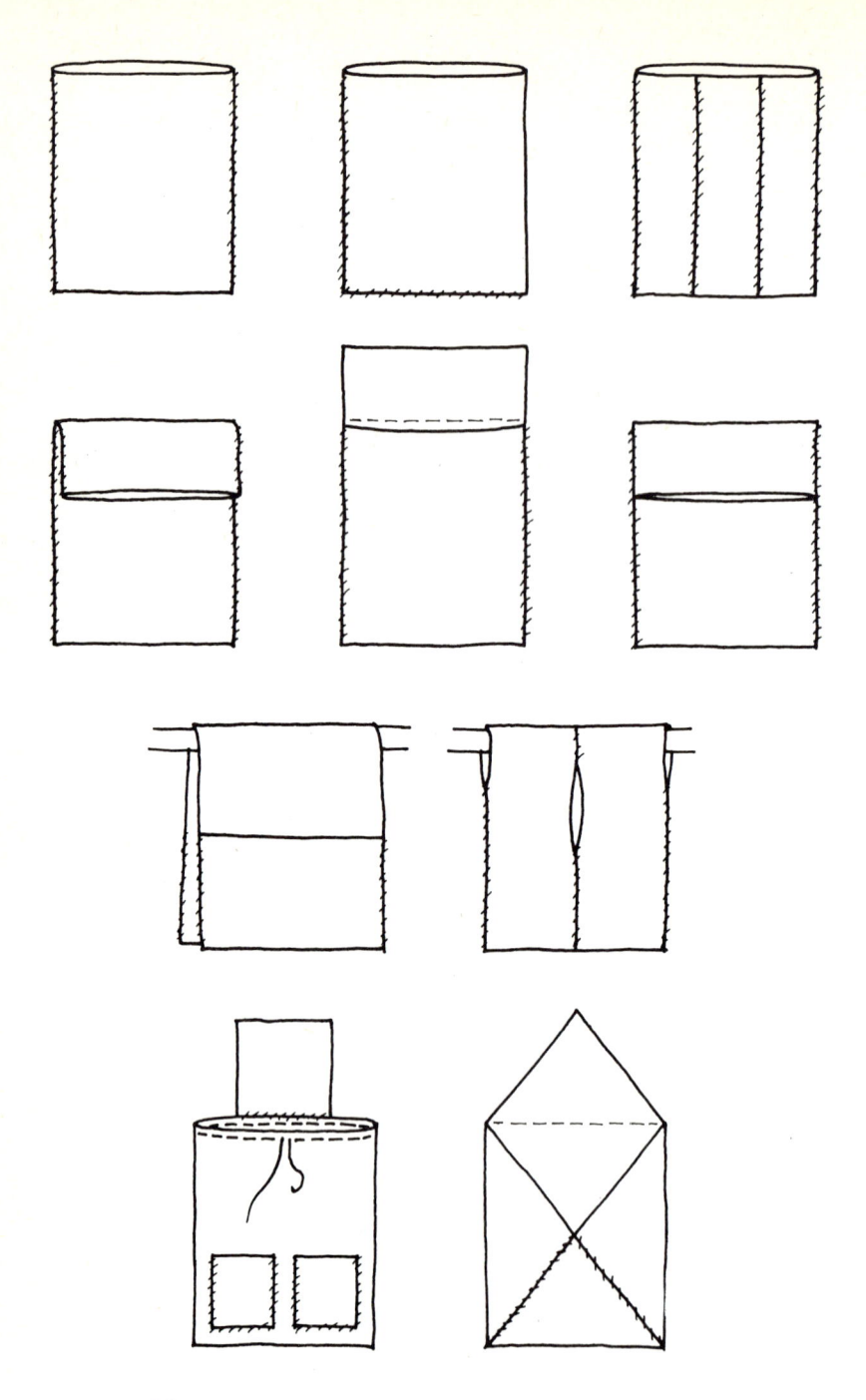

Figure 109. Handbags—general features of form.

PLANNING AND MAKING

The planning of the job can start with the following choices:
What requirements should the handbag meet?
Which type shall I choose?
Which material(s) and equipment shall I choose?
What type of decoration shall I choose?
When it is a matter of planning a practical article for every-day use like a handbag, it is reasonable to make choices in the above-mentioned order, i.e., to begin with the question of form. But it is important to stress the need to stop other choices conflicting with the choice of form; instead they should support it. If the function of the handbag is intended to be that of a piece of jewellery, the considerations will, as a rule, take colour and composition as their starting point—and bring about a more imaginative approach in the working process.

When the work has been planned, the form is made in soft paper, adjusted if necessary, and joined together so that the proportions of the spatial shape can be judged.

In the same way one experiments with the composition by drawing it on a sheet of paper and observing how the components mutually affect each other. The rough outlines of the colour combination can also be decided on at this stage, whereas the structure of the material in relation to decoration has to be tested using the actual yarn or fabric directly.

We are now in a position to fill in the diagram, to experiment and to make decisions on technical details, and to start making the bag, making adjustments while doing so. Finish off with an evaluation of product and process in relation to aims.

Measurement diagrams

These diagrams are for noting down body measurements and calculating basic measurements to be used when drawing the three basic shapes (see pages 73, 81, and 82).

THE TIGHT-FITTING BASIC SHAPE I

Body measurements	Calculations	Basic measurements
Width of body		Width of body
Width of arm		Width of sleeve
Length		Length of body
Wing span		Length of sleeve
Width round the neck		Diameter of neckhole
Width round the head		Breadth of hood
Double height of head		Height of hood

THE LOOSE BASIC SHAPE II

Body measurements	Calculations	Basic measurements
Width of body		Width of body
Width of arm		Width of sleeve
Length		Length of body
Wing span		Length of sleeve

THE WIDE BASIC SHAPE III

Body measurements	Calculations	Basic measurements
Width of body		Width of body
Width of arm		Width of sleeve
Length		Length of body
Wing span		Length of sleeve

Index

Abyssinian tunic, 41
Afghanistan: caftan, 54
  handbag, 108
African tunics, 41, 42
Ainokimono, 64
Albanian: tunic, 41
  waistcoat, 66
Anorak, 43–8, 68
  variation, 102–3
Arabian: aba, 22, 28
  jibba, 22
  waistcoat, 66
Armholes, 86, 90

Basic shape(s): body
  measurements, 17, 74, 112
    classification, 12–14
    drawing, 73–82
    drawing variations, 90–105
    flat and three-dimensional, 15–16
    function, 72
    variations, 83–9
    wide, loose and tight-fitting, 72, 80–81, 112
Birket-Smith, Kai, 9
Blouse, 72
  Bronze Age, 33–7, 68, 96–7
  Inca, 29, 31
  tunic variation, 99
Body measurements, 17, 67, 74–7, 82
  diagrams for 3 basic shapes, 80–81, 112
Body proportions, Leonardo's diagram of, 11
Borneo handbag, 108
Broby-Johansen, 9
Bronze Age blouse and skirt, 33–7, 67–8, 96–7
Bronze Age burial mounds, 33

Caftan, 13, 14, 49, 50, 52–8, 67, 68, 88
  Chinese, 55–6
  Egyptian, 57–8

fastenings, 53
variations, 103–4
Canadian child's skirt, 37
Cape, 14
Casings shirts, 46
Chinese: caftan, 53, 55–6
  waistcoat, 66
Cloak, 12, 13, 14
Coats, 38, 41–2, 49, 72
Collars, 89, 92, 94, 95

Decoration of clothes, 67
Denmark: Egtved girl's garment and grave, 33–5
  Huldre bog peplus, 19, 21, 22, 24, 68
  tunics, 41, 42
Dress (tunic variation), 101

Egtved girl's garment and grave, 33–5
Egyptian: caftan, 55, 57–8
  loincloth, 19
  tunic, 41
Eskimo anorak, 43–9

Fibula (dress pin), 22
Finnish tunic, 41
Flap, 88, 94, 95
Front openings, 88, 95
Function: of basic shape, 72
  of clothes, 9–10, 67–71

Gathers, 84, 92
Greek peplus, 21–2, 23, 67
Gundestrup vessel, 21
Gussets, 87–8, 90, 95

Hald, Margrethe, 76
Handbags, fabric, 106–11
Hansen, Henny Harald, 49
Hatt, Gudmund, 93
Hood, 79–80, 82, 89, 93, 94, 95
Huldre bog peplus, 19, 21, 22, 24, 68
Hungarian tunic, 42

113

Inca blouse, 29, 31
Indian: caftan, 53, 54
    handbag, 108
    sari, 19
    tunics, 41, 42
Indonesian waistcoat, 66
Iranian: blouse, 37
    tunic, 41

Japanese: handbag, 107
    kimono, 50, 59–64, 67
    socks, 62
Jellaba, 13, 14, 22, 25–8
    variation, 97–8
Jibba, 22, 28
Judo jacket, 64

Kanga, 18–19, 20, 67, 95
    variation, 96
Kayak anorak, 45
Kimono, Japanese, 50, 59–64, 67
Kirtle, 38
Korean caftan, 53, 54
Kurdistan waistcoat, 66

Length of garments, 84, 91–2
Leonardo da Vinci, 11
Loincloth, Egyptian, 19
Looms: circular, 19
    loin, 26

Macedonian waistcoat, 66
Manufacture of fabrics, 68
Mexican: handbag, 108
    ponchos, 32
Mongolian caftan, 53, 54
Moroccan jellaba, 26

Neckholes, 73, 78–9, 82, 88–9, 92–3, 94, 95
Norsemen, 44–5
North African: handbag, 108
    jellaba, 22, 25
    jibba, 28
North American: handbag, 108
    tunic, 42
Norwegian handbag, 108

Obi, Japanese, 50

Palestinian tunic, 41

Peplus, 19, 21–5, 95
    Greek, 21–2, 23, 67
    Huldre bog, 19, 21, 22, 24
    variation, 96
Peruvian: handbag, 108
    mummy case, 30
    poncho, 29, 31, 32
Pleats, 92, 93
Poncho, 12, 13, 14, 25–6, 29, 31–2
    variation, 96

Red oil bottle, 23
Roman toga and tunic, 19, 38
Rumanian tunic, 42
Russian: handbag, 108
    tunics, 41, 42
    waistcoat, 66

Serbian tunic, 42
Shirt: casings, 46
    tunic variation, 100
Shoulder piece, 84
Silk route, 49, 51
Skirts, 67
    Bronze age, 33, 35
Sleeves, 73, 75, 77, 84–7, 94, 95
Social status and clothes, 49, 67
South American ponchos, 32
Spanish: bolero, 66
    tunic, 42
Sudanese tunic, 41
Swedish waistcoat, 66

Tanzanian kanga, 18, 19
Tibetan: caftan, 54
    ponchos, 32
    tunic, 41
    waistcoat, 66
Tilke, Max, 13, 22
Toga, Roman, 19, 38
Tunics, 13, 14, 18, 38–42, 67, 72
    variations, 99–101
Turkestan tunic, 41
Turkish: caftan, 55
    handbag, 108
    tunic, 42
    waistcoat, 66

Waistcoat, 65–6, 72
    variation, 104–5

Water skins, skin garments,
  Eskimo, 45, 46
Width: calculation of extra, 80–81
  of garments, 84, 91–2
  of material, 15, 68, 69–70, 83, 87

Wingspan, 76, 77
Wraparound garments, 12, 13, 18, 22

Yoke, 84, 94
Yugoslav tunic, 38

Notes and measurements

Notes and measurements

Notes and measurements

Notes and measurements

Notes and measurements